TALKIN

THE INTERNET

Herbie Brennan

Cover illustration by
Mark Thomas

SCHOLASTIC

*For Sean Ryan, who got me back on the Net
against all odds.*

Scholastic Children's Books,
Commonwealth House, 1-19 New Oxford Street
London WC1A 1NU, UK
A division of Scholastic Ltd
London ~ New York ~ Toronto ~ Sydney ~ Auckland

Published in the UK by Scholastic Ltd, 1998
Text copyright © Herbie Brennan, 1998
Cover illustration copyright © Mark Thomas, 1998

ISBN 0 590 19400 3
All rights reserved

Typeset by Rapid Reprographics Ltd
Printed by Cox and Wyman Ltd, Reading, Berks.

10 9 8 7 6 5 4 3 2 1

The right of Herbie Brennan and Mark Thomas to be identified as the author and
illustrator of this work has been asserted by them in accordance with the Copyright,
Designs and Patents Act, 1988.

This book is sold subject to the condition that it shall not, by way of trade or otherwise
be lent, resold, hired out, or otherwise circulated without the publisher's prior consent in
any form of binding or cover other than that in which it is published and without a similar
condition, including this condition, being imposed upon the subsequent purchaser.

Contents

Section One: What's happening?
Site 1: Talking to God   11

Section Two: So you want to surf the Net?
Site 2: Getting on the Net   17
Site 3: What is the Internet?   18
Site 4: Aladdin's electronic cave   20
Site 5: Using the Net   23

Section Three: The hardware and the software
Site 6: The computer you need   27
Site 7: Mysterious modem   29
Site 8: Your service provider   33
Site 9: Protocol   35
Site 10: The software you'll need   36
Site 11: The software you'll get   38
Site 12: Plug-ins and helpers   40

Section Four: What you can do on the Net
Site 13: E-mail   43
Site 14: Illicit e-mail   46
Site 15: World Wide Web   48
Site 16: Newsgroups   52
Site 17: Useful newsgroups   56
Site 18: Setting up your own   58
Site 19: Netspeak   60
Site 20: Netiquette   63

Site 21: Emoticons	66
Site 22: Chat	68

Section Five: Is the Net a murderous monster?

Site 23: The first 'Internet'	75
Site 24: Luddites	76
Site 25: Frankenstein technology	77
Site 26: Technology that turned	79
Site 27: Electronic democracy?	81

Section Six: Genesis

Site 28: How it started	85
Site 29: Who's in control?	92
Site 30: Net customs	95
Site 31: Flame wars	97

Section Seven: Things you can find on the Net

Site 32: Fishing with the Net	103
Site 33: Finding what you want	105

Section Eight: Things that might find you on the Net

Site 34: The plague pit	109
Site 35: Masters of Deception	111
Site 36: Cyberwar	116

Section Nine: Other Net Nasties and how to avoid them

Site 37: Romantic encounter	121

Site 38: Sex crimes	126
Site 39: Legislation and the Net	130
Site 40: Safe surfing	133
Site 41: The case against censorship	137

Section Ten: Dangerous adventures
Site 42: A brief history of MUD	143
Site 43: Playing in the MUD	145
Site 44: Sticking in the MUD	147
Site 45: Heroine addiction	149
Site 46: Sinking in the MUD	152
Site 47: Internet addiction	157

Section Eleven: Coming soon
Site 48: The future of the Net	161
Site 49: Virtual reality	163
Site 50: Ultimate interface	168
Site 51: Passport to Cyberia	172
Site 52: Alternative futures	174
Site 53: Future perfect	176
Site 54: Future imperfect	179
Site 55: Future possible	182

Section Twelve: It's make your mind up time
| **Site 56:** Decision Day | 187 |
| **Site 57:** The last word | 190 |

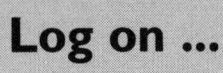

Log on ...

Important: Read This First

You can enjoy this book the ordinary way. By starting at the beginning and reading to the end.

And because it's laid out in sites, you can skip a section if it deals with something you already know.

But there's a new and different way you can read this book.

The way you surf the Net.

By following hypertext links.

On **World Wide Web** P.48, certain words are underlined. You click on them to find out more.

Since you can't click in a book, the underlined words have a page number after them. To find out more, just turn to that page.

This means you can learn about the Internet the way you want to.

Following up the threads that interest you.

Forming your opinions as you go along.

And getting in some surfing practice in preparation for the real thing.

The Internet

WHAT'S HAPPENING?

Site 1 — Talking to God

▶ Here's how to talk to God.

First, dial up the **World Wide Web**[P.48] and go to: *http://www.primenet.com/~prayers*

Next, decide what you want to say to God, write it down and send it (in the first instance) to Prayers Heavenbound.

The reason you should do so, according to this World Wide Web page, is that:

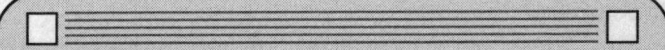

> 'Modern technology has finally caught up with mankind's spiritual needs. Here is a non-denominational, publicly accessible direct link to the Heavens that can electronically beam prayers, hopes and dreams into space, into time ... into for ever.'
>
> 'Prayers, especially thankful ones, are often published as advertisements in newspapers, but we have to say (with no disrespect) that there is not much evidence that God subscribes to daily newspapers.' – quoted from the Prayers Heavenbound Web page.

Prayers Heavenbound optical scanner accepts both letters and drawings and a specialist computer transforms them into digital pulses which modulate a microwave transmitter. The transmitter then beams the information at the speed of light via satellite into deep space. There the messages 'become available to be intercepted by God'.

THE INTERNET

Is this WWW page for real? They charge you money, give an 'unprecedented lifetime guarantee' and mail you a Broadcast Certificate, so it must be.

Prayers Heavenbound is only one of literally millions of Net sites. There are others that will fascinate, astonish, amuse, annoy, perhaps even disgust you. You'll find all of them on the Net. You'll find some of them in this book.

If you're one of those readers who do what they're told, you'll already have noted you can tackle the book itself two ways. You can read it or you can surf it.

Either way, you'll need to know a bit about the way it's structured.

First, the whole thing is divided up into twelve sections, each one very roughly equivalent to a chapter in an ordinary book.

Within those broad sections you'll find sites. Each site is like a page on the **World Wide Web**^{P.48}. It covers a single topic related to life on the Net.

If you're surfing the book, you'll probably do most of your jumping between sites. If you're reading it the good old-fashioned way you'll move through the sites section by section.

As you do so, you'll notice that the first four sections are sort of technical. They deal with the hardware and software you'll need to get on the Net and the basics of what you'll find when you get there.

But after that there's a change. After the first four sections, you'll start getting information on the pros and cons of the Internet, on the good things and the bad.

This gets rolling with the discussion in section 5 on **Frankenstein technology**^{P.77}, and continues with the sort of detail you'll need to make up your mind about the one question everybody's asking these days:

Will the Internet change things for the better or the worse?

WHAT'S HAPPENING?

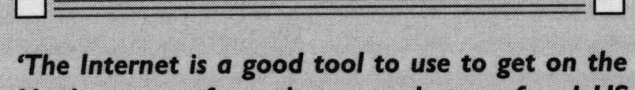

'The Internet is a good tool to use to get on the Net.' – quote from the somewhat confused US Presidential candidate Bob Dole.

Nobody doubts the Internet will bring change. When you read the **How it started** P.85 section, you'll see how the process has begun already. But where is it going? Where will it end? And how will you be affected?

You can rely on one thing. Even though this site began with Talking to God, you won't get preached at in this book. What you'll get is the information and opinions (for and against) that will let you form your own judgements.

That way you'll avoid some of the wilder misconceptions about the Internet. Like the idea that every **World Wide Web** P.48 page is filled with porn. Or the notion that the Internet is open to everybody everywhere. Or even that astonishing opinion in the box above, voiced by the man who was looking for the most powerful job on the planet ... but (maybe fortunately) didn't get it.

Good reading. And good surfing.

Site 2 — Getting on the Net

▶Getting on the Internet is easy.
You attach your computer to a **modem** P.29.
You attach your modem to a phone line.
You attach your phone line to a **service provider** P.33.
Your service provider links you to the Net.
It's all so easy and it seems like everybody's doing it. But you might ask yourself one question:
Do you really want to?

If you wonder why you mightn't want to join the Net Site 37 ▶

The Internet

What is the Internet?

▶ A computer network is a series of individual computers linked together by cables or telephone lines so they can communicate with each other. Sit at the keyboard of one computer in a network and you can send information to another, get information back, or even run applications programs at a distance.

The Internet is a network that draws together existing networks set up by schools, businesses, the military and so on into a sort of super-network. This super-network is based on a common way of communicating known as a **protocol** P.35.

Amateur radio, cable television wires, spread spectrum radio, satellite, and fibre optics are all used to deliver Internet services, but the most common medium is the telephone line.

How it started P.85 is complicated, but since its creation in 1983 the Internet has grown enormously.

By the end of 1991, it had 700,000 host computers — that's to say computers holding information that can be accessed by others in the network. The number of actual computers linked in, most of them PCs, was more like 4 million. Over 36 countries were on board. There were at least 5,000 sub-networks within the big one.

> *The Internet is spreading faster than fax machines, faster than portable telephones, faster than computer games.*

From 1991 to June 1994, the number of hosts jumped again from 700,000 to 2.3 million. By November the same year, it had gone up to 3,864,000. The number of countries on board was over 80.

SO YOU WANT TO SURF THE NET?

In 1996 there were 37 million people with access to the Internet in North America (that's USA and Canada) alone. 24 million had used the Net in the past three months. 18 million had used the **World Wide Web** P.48.

> According to a recent survey, half of all Internet users have come on line in the last year.

In 1994, the number of companies registered on the Internet was 14,726. One of them, Exxon, had links in 261 networks. By 1996, there were more than 10 million US businesses with Internet links. Some 15,379 of them had **World Wide Web** P.48 sites at the start of the year and more were coming aboard at the rate of 73 a day.

> 'The Internet unites people worldwide through a simple computer screen. It is cheaper than using the telephone and can be far more interesting than a TV set.'
> Kelly, 15

The Internet worldwide was growing at the rate of 20 per cent per month. That's something like 10 *million* new clients every thirty days. Unless it slows down, everybody on the planet will be on line by the year 2003.

Or will they? Site 27 ▶

THE INTERNET

Site 4 — Aladdin's electronic cave

►Millions of Internet computers store files. By linking with them, you can get into those files. It's like wandering into Aladdin's electronic cave. Everything you've ever dreamed about is there.

> '*No ambition, however extravagant, no fantasy, however outlandish, can any longer be dismissed as crazy or impossible. This is the age when you can finally do it all. Suddenly technology has given us powers with which we can manipulate not only the physical world but also ourselves. You can become whatever you want to be.*'
> Ed Regis, on Extropians
> http://www.hotwired.com/wired2.10/features/extropians.html

Files come in different types.

First of all, there are text files. Whatever you want to read about is there.

You want to learn how to fix a puncture on your bike? It's there, on file. You want to know how to make jewellery? It's there. You want to find out how to pick locks, adjust your satellite dish, bake a chocolate cake, cheat at poker? It's all there. You want the low-down on your favourite band? It's there in forty different languages.

Everybody's dumping stuff into the Internet, on every subject you can think of from aeronautics to Zen. Universities are converting whole libraries into electronic files for distribution on the Net. There's one university in

America that's working on 100,000 books printed over the past century on bridges, roads and public works. Another in the UK is concentrating on psychology papers and textbooks.

Thousands of authors, professional and amateur, post their work on the Net. There are children's stories, detective stories, romance stories, short stories, long stories, novels, whole encyclopaedias.

The next sort of files are picture files. These come in a variety of formats – **GIF**[P.61] (Graphic Interchange Format), **JPEG** [P.61] (a compressed graphic format) and so on – but the bottom line is that they're pictures of some sort – black and white or colour photographs, cartoons, paintings, line drawings, sketches, blueprints, architectural drawings, icons, illustrations, fractals and other computer-generated images.

What's in these pictures? Like the text files, the answer is *everything* – complete deck plans for the Starship *Enterprise*, photographs of Venus, weird drawings by Escher, blurred shots of flying saucers, people with no clothes on, elephants and teddy bears, rain forests at sunset, the latest sighting of the Loch Ness monster.

> *If you can see it in your mind, you can see it on the Net.*

Sound files run all the way from Arnie saying 'I'll be back' to puking noises. You can find music and sound effects and Leonard Nimmoy doing the whole *Space, the Final Frontier* intro to the first Star Trek series.

Movies on the Net are movie snippets – somebody talking to you about the latest product ... a sports personality saying a few words ... an animated cartoon. Depending on your computer set-up, the quality on replay will vary from poor to middling.

Finally, there are software files. Whatever your computer, the Internet is beyond doubt your biggest single source of software in the world. Games, spreadsheets, word-processors, graphic viewers, paint programs, calendars, organizers, utilities, system extensions, databases, communications programs ... until you dive in, you won't believe how much software is sitting waiting for you.

Most of it is either totally free, or yours to try out free for a limited time – and now that recordable CD systems are coming on the market at increasingly reasonable prices, you'll have plenty of space to store them.

More about freebies Site 11 ▶
Sites of interest Site 56 ▶

So you want to surf the Net?

Site 5 — Using the Net

▶ You've linked your **computer** P.27 to a few million other computers and consequently put yourself in touch with several billion **files** P.20 containing text, sounds, music, movies and software. Many of them contain a mixture. Movie files will normally have both sound and pictures. Software files frequently have text, sound, pictures and animations. There are whole electronic magazines (called e-zines) published on the Net with as rich a mix of material as the software.

Any file you can reach, you can download. When you download a file, what you actually do is make an electronic copy of it. The original file stays where it is. The copy is saved on to your hard disk (or a convenient floppy) for you to use at your leisure.

Sometimes, of course, you won't want to download the whole file. The Internet is chock-a-block with information sources – encyclopaedias, textbooks, references of every description. Most of the time all you need is a particular bit of information from these sources. You search it out and download just that.

The Internet doesn't end with computers and files. If you attach a digital camera to an Internet computer anybody who makes the link can see what that camera is pointing at.

> '*I think the Net is a fast way to get information and make friends.*'
> **Nicola, 11**

THE INTERNET

If you have **IRC** P.68 software, you can chat with other users by typing what you want to say on your keyboard and watching their response come up on screen.

There's technology that allows you to have verbal conversations with other surfers, even using a relatively slow (14.4) **modem** P.29. This technology effectively turns the Net into an international telephone system that charges you only for a local call.

When people find they can communicate with one another, it's human nature to clump into groups of similar interests. That's exactly what happened on the Net. The groupings are called 'newsgroups'. Each one is a sort of electronic club set up to discuss a particular topic. **Newsgroups** P.52 are like files – they cover every subject you could imagine.

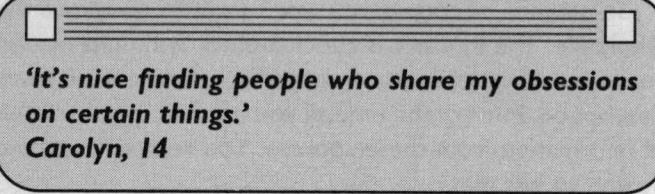

'It's nice finding people who share my obsessions on certain things.'
Carolyn, 14

So, by joining the Internet you've linked yourself to a few million other computers, given yourself access to a few billion files and put yourself in a position to talk to several million people anywhere on earth about the things that most interest you.

If you're sociable there's more on newsgroups Site 16 ▶
And on Internet chat Site 22 ▶

Section Three
THE HARDWARE AND THE SOFTWARE

THE HARDWARE AND THE SOFTWARE

Site 6 — The computer you need

▶ The original Internet computers were all mainframes and supercomputers. They're still linked in, but you don't need anything like that firepower.

Almost any personal computer manufactured in the past five years is suitable for linking to the Net. If your machine is older, don't despair. The chances are you'll still be able to link in.

The critical thing is whether your computer has a modem port – a place where you can plug in a modem.

> *'The Net will mean that different people from all over the world can communicate and learn. It brings us closer to other countries and gives us more views on things.'*
> **Giovanna, 16**

Check round the back or look it up in the manual. If you've got a modem port, you're in business. Even if you *haven't* got a modem port, you're probably still in business. Your computer will certainly have a printer port and with a bit of a fiddle, you can usually persuade the software to drive a modem through that instead.

But while you *can* join the Internet with just about any clunky old piece of computer hardware, for comfort and enjoyment, you'll really need at least a 486 SX25 IBM PC or compatible with 8 megabytes of on-board RAM. A Pentium processor is nice, but not necessary.

It doesn't have to be an IBM, of course. The equivalent power in an Atari, Amiga or whatever else you may have sitting in your room will do nicely.

In fact, so will anything in the Macintosh 68030 series or above. A Mac will give you more of what you need since all Macs have sound capabilities as standard. If you're using one of the others and want to hear the music, you may have to shell out for a separate sound card.

You may even have to shell out for a separate video card as well.

Modem advice Site 7 ▶
Your service provider Site 8 ▶
What software you need Site 10 ▶
What extra software you'll need Site 12 ▶

THE HARDWARE AND THE SOFTWARE

Site 7 — Mysterious modem

▶ If you tie two empty tin cans together, pull the string tight and talk into one of them, your friend can hear what you're saying if he puts his ear to the other.

The reason this happens is that when you talk, you set up vibrations in the air. The tin can picks them up and passes them along the string, making the can on the far end vibrate in the same way. This causes more vibrations in the air, which your friend's ear picks up as sound waves.

What happens when you talk down a telephone is a bit different. The electronics in the mouthpiece translate the sound vibrations of your voice into electrical pulses which are then sent down the phone line. More electronics in the earpiece at the far end translate these pulses back into sound vibrations so the person you're calling can hear you.

That's how your phone works at its most basic — electrical pulses down a copper wire. In a lot of places for a lot of calls, it gets more complicated. Some phone systems have now replaced copper wire with fibre-optic cable so the electrical pulses have to be turned into light. Many long-distance calls now go via satellite, so the pulses have to be turned into radio waves. All phone calls go through exchanges, most controlled by computers, a few by real live people, and are shunted about all over the place.

But the bottom line remains the same. You talk this end and the machines translate one form of communication (sound waves) into another (electrical pulses, light pulses, radio waves) which can be pumped quickly to their destination for reassembly into sound waves.

The whole process gets a lot more interesting when you want your computer to talk down the phone.

Computers work with digital information. They manage

everything they do, from word-processing to **game playing** P.143, by manipulating streams of information made up entirely of zeros and ones. So when you want to pass digital computer information down a phone line, you need to find something that will translate it into the sort of electrical pulses the phone system carries.

The 'something' you need is called a modem.

> As a rule of thumb, you should buy the fastest modem you can afford in order to make an Internet connection.

Modems are boxes that plug into your computer at one end and your phone line at the other. They do for your computer exactly what your telephone handset does for your voice. They translate one form of communication into another.

You can get very technical about modems. You can talk about **protocols** P.35, handshaking, XON, XOFF and so forth, but 99 per cent of this stuff you don't need to know because it's handled by the software that comes with your modem. The important thing is that a modem lets your computer talk down a phone line. If a computer at the far end has a modem too, then it can listen. You can listen to the data stream yourself, using an ordinary telephone handset, but all you hear is a high-pitched chattering whine. You need a modem and a computer to make sense of it.

THE HARDWARE AND THE SOFTWARE

> *'The Net will be a vital part of my future. I think that by the time I reach college, a lot of my tutors will be posting assignments, references, etc. And there's going to be a lot of information exchanged, things like doctor's appointments, paying bills... Oh, and movies and music.'*
> **Carolyn, 15**

The smallest unit of information a computer handles is known as a *bit*. Modem speed is measured in *bps* which stands for *bits per second* – the number of bits the box can pump down the phone line in a clock tick.

It takes ten bits for your computer to create just one letter of the alphabet or one digit of a number. The paragraph you're reading now contains 234 characters. So your computer would use 2,340 bits to transfer it down the phone line.

However powerful your computer, it's your modem that controls how fast the transfer takes place. If your modem runs at, say, 2400 bps, it will take about a second to push the paragraph through. That doesn't sound much, but you're only talking about a single paragraph – and a short one at that. To transfer a whole page, a 2400 bps modem will take about eight seconds. That's a long time when you're sitting staring at a screen.

Text is the fastest thing you can move. If you want to push pictures, sounds, software or movies down a phone line, you're talking about hundreds of thousands, sometimes hundreds of millions of bits.

As a general rule of thumb, you should always use the fastest modem you can afford for an Internet connection and in any case avoid any modem designated lower than 14.4. (The figure translates to 14,400 bps.) It's possible to connect with less, but everything will happen in slow motion and the phone bills will be enormous. Even at 14,400 bps, you can spend an hour or more downloading software.

◀(Site 6) **The computer that goes with it**
Your service provider (Site 8)▶
What software you need (Site 10)▶
What extra software you'll need (Site 12)▶

THE HARDWARE AND THE SOFTWARE

Site 8 — **Your service provider**

▶In the bad old days, the only way you could get on to the Net was to know a scientist or a general who'd let you link with their computer. Today there are companies called service providers whose sole function is to provide you with a gateway to the Internet.

There are two main types of service provider. One is the net within the Net. CompuServe is a typical example of this type. It has its own magazine, forums, libraries, software and services. You can spend many enjoyable and productive hours on CompuServe without ever going near the Internet. But if it's the Internet you want, you can get there through CompuServe – at time of writing they offer several hours connection time each month at no additional cost.

The other sort of provider is much more straightforward. It just plugs you into the Internet. Its local services are limited or non-existent. (Although many providers are starting to introduce or extend local services in order to attract new customers.)

Both types of service provider charge money to take you on board. In Britain and Ireland, this tends to be a flat fee. In places like North America or Australia, they usually work it by time – the longer you stay on the Net, the more you pay.

Wherever you are, major subnets like CompuServe will have a range of charges, some of them time-based. However, just about everybody will give you the **software** P.36 you need free.

Having paid your service provider, your only other worry is what your folks will say about the phone bill.

The Internet

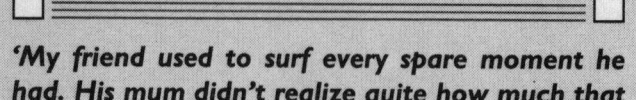

> YOU DON'T HAVE TO BE RICH TO BE WELL CONNECTED — *headline on an ad for a UK Internet service provider.*

In the UK calls are timed, so the longer you stay connected, the higher the phone bill is going to be. Fortunately the UK has a *lot* of service providers so the chances are you can find one with a local call.

In places like Australia and North America call charges are often fixed, so the phone bill is less of a concern. And in many places there's a chance that your service provider will offer a toll-free or local-rate number.

> 'My friend used to surf every spare moment he had. His mum didn't realize quite how much that was – she had a fit when she saw the phone bill.'
> Ian, 13

How do you find a good service provider? Any one of the numerous Internet magazines in your local newsagent's will carry provider ads and some will publish editorial listings showing the benefits offered by different companies.

You're also likely to find service provider advertisements in your favourite computer magazine as well.

◀ Site 6 **Computer advice**
◀ Site 7 **Modem advice**

THE HARDWARE AND THE SOFTWARE

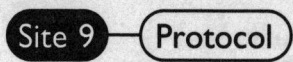
Site 9 — Protocol

▶ If there was one thing that helped the Internet grow like a mushroom, it was the introduction in the middle 1970s of an ingenious new system called the TCP/IP standard.

TCP stands for Transmission Control Protocol, which is the way messages are turned into electronic packets for transmission and back into messages at the far end.

IP stands for Internet Protocol, which helps the packet get where it needs to go, even across different systems.

The point about this protocol is that it allows you to link into the Internet whatever way your computer works. If the Internet is a Network of networks, TCP/IP is a Protocol of protocols.

Your local **service provider** P.33 will supply you with the **software** P.36 you need to link into this master protocol.

◀ Site 8 **Your service provider**
The necessary software Site 10 ▶
And a few extras Site 12 ▶

THE INTERNET

Site 10 — The software you'll need

➤Once you're linked to the Net, there are a number of things you can do.

You can send and receive **e-mail** P.43.

You can download games and other goodies on to your hard disk.

You can access **newsgroups** P.52 and **chat lines** P.68.

You can surf the **World Wide Web** P.48.

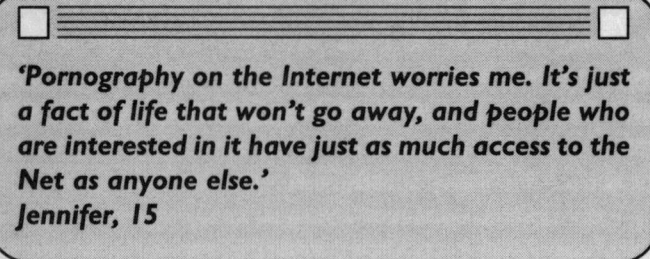

'Pornography on the Internet worries me. It's just a fact of life that won't go away, and people who are interested in it have just as much access to the Net as anyone else.'
Jennifer, 15

All these activities require special software, but the chances are your **service provider** P.33 will give you all you need for free.

If they don't, find a friend who already has an Internet connection and borrow his system for an hour. You'll find all the software you can handle waiting for you on the Net. You can download it through the phone line on to a floppy disk ... again for free.

THE HARDWARE AND THE SOFTWARE

> 'You grow old fast in the computer business, then you're laughed at, then you die.' – journalist Bryan Appleyard in an article on Netscape author Marc Andreessen who created the **browser** P.39 software that made him millions while still in his teens.

And if you don't have a friend with a connection, you *still* aren't going to have to pay. Search your local newsagent for computer magazines that have free CD-ROMS or floppies on the cover. Over and over you'll find these disks contain Internet software ... for free.

To begin with, you will probably confine yourself to an e-mail package like Eudora and a Web browser like Netscape Navigator, Mosaic or Internet Explorer. Most Web **browsers** P.39 allow you to connect to **newsgroups** P.52 as well as the **World Wide Web** P.48 itself. Many of the more recent versions have e-mail capabilities too.

Extra software you'll need   Site 12 ▶

THE INTERNET

Site 11 — The software you'll get

➤ There are three broad categories of software available on the Net.

First, there's the familiar commercial software. Some businesses have begun to advertise and market their software on the Internet. To protect themselves against thieves, they'll normally set up a firewall – a stand-alone computer that vets all incoming Internet communications and stops you from getting your hands on protected data.

Commercial programs are kept in locked **files** P.20 on the Internet. To unlock them, you usually give the supplier a credit card number. He debits the account, gives you a code to unlock the file and you download the program. The manual comes with it in a text file.

Next there's public domain software, or freeware as it's often called. Freeware is software that's free. There are people out there who spend months, even years, creating interesting, useful, ingenious software then give it away. You can download freebies at no cost whatsoever, use it as long and as often as you want. You can pass copies on to your friends.

> *The only thing that's missing from Net software is the fancy box. Sometimes it's cheaper to buy your software this way, because the publisher saves on packaging.*

Finally, there's shareware. Shareware is commercial software distributed on the honour system. You get it without paying. You're allowed to use it for a limited time to find out how it works and if you really want it. But at the end of that time – which can be anything up to three months or more – you are honour bound to send payment

THE HARDWARE AND THE SOFTWARE

to the person who created it.

Usually the cost of shareware is a lot less than the cost of a comparable commercial program.

One of the most bizarre developments is the fact that many commercial publishers manage to make money by giving away their products via the Net. The **Web** P.48 browser Navigator was a pioneer of this approach.

At its most simple, a Web browser is a program that lets you access the **World Wide Web** P.48 and move from site to site within it. It will normally have facilities to download software, save Web pages or files and keep a note of where you've been during your current surfing session. More advanced browsers have **e-mail** P.43 and **newsgroup** P.52 facilities as well.

Netscape offer Navigator to buy in the normal way, boxed and with a printed manual. You can place your order over the Net and the package is shipped by post.

Alternatively, you can download the product direct through your modem with the manual included in a text file. Since you've paid, you're a registered user and can get technical assistance and back-up when you need it.

But alongside this completely orthodox approach, Netscape also allow you to download Navigator without paying anything. Maybe this is supposed to be shareware, where you're supposed to pay something eventually, but they don't say so. And it certainly isn't freeware either, since Navigator is very much a copyright product. What it feels like is a gift from Netscape to you.

The approach looked like commercial suicide when it was first tried, but while millions gratefully accepted the gift, millions more registered and paid. And Netscape took control of the entire Web browser market.

Of the 40 million who cruise the Web at time of writing, 85 per cent are using Navigator.

THE INTERNET

Site 12 — Plug-ins and helpers

▶Browsers browse, which means they get you to the sites you'd like to see, but they don't necessarily do all you want when you get there.

The problem is that more and more Net sites are adding fancy bells and whistles – movies, sounds, animations – that the browser isn't equipped to process.

As the multimedia aspect of the Net expanded, software engineers were faced with a dilemma. If they expanded their browsers to match, the applications would become too unwieldy to fit the RAM of the average PC. So they opted for another approach. Most browsers make use of things called *plug-ins* and *helpers*.

A plug-in is an optional piece of software you can install in your browser to handle a specific job. A helper is a totally separate program the browser calls on when it's needed. Once on your hard disk and listed in the browser's memory, the plug-in pops up like a genie each time the browser visits a site that uses its technology.

If you elect to cruise without plug-ins – possible but inadvisable – your browser will frequently alert you to the fact that it's come up against an 'unknown file type'. Many Web designers are kind enough to build in details of the plug-in you need and where to get it, so your browser often tells you that as well.

But adding plug-ins becomes a sort of madness after a while. There are so many of them available. And, unlike helpers which just take up disk space, plug-ins fatten your browser.

◀ Site 10 **For your software basics**

Section Four
WHAT YOU CAN DO ON THE NET

WHAT YOU CAN DO ON THE NET

Site 13 — E-mail

► The 'e' in e-mail stands for electronic.

To send a letter e-mail, you run your e-mail software then type in your message and the address you want it to reach.

An e-mail address is different from a postal address, although in a peculiar sort of way it follows the same format. A typical postal address might be:

Elizabeth Windsor, 222 Any Street, Dublin, Ireland.

The same person's e-mail address might be something like this:

liz@iol.ie

Although they look very different, they break down in much the same way. In the postal address you have the name of the person, followed by their location, followed by the country they live in.

> *'I think the Internet will stop all snail mail.'*
> **Shauna, 15**

In the e-mail address, the bit before '@' is the name of the person you're sending to, usually in an abbreviated form: *liz* stands for 'Elizabeth Windsor'.

The '@' itself stands for at.

The bit between the @ and the full stop is the name of the **service provider**[P.33] where you'll find Liz's electronic post-box. In the example, 'iol' stands for the service provider Ireland On-Line.

The letters after the full stop are code for the country. The letters 'ie' stand for Ireland. If the address was in

Sweden, the letters would be 'se'. England, Scotland, Wales and Northern Ireland carry the letters 'uk'.

If there's no country code on the address you're using, you can take it the recipient lives in America. In that case, you'll probably find the letters 'com' or 'org' at the end. This dates back to the time in **Internet history** P.85 when US networks joining the Net slotted themselves into six basic categories, known as domains. These categories were (and still are): Military, Educational, Government, Commercial, Organizations and Networking; and they are denoted by the abbreviations 'mil', 'edu', 'gov', 'com', 'org' and 'net'.

'Com' denotes a commercial operation, a business that's joined the Net, including service provider businesses. Org covers all the non-profit groups like churches, charities, clubs and so on.

Once you've finished and addressed your message, a click of your computer mouse sends it winging through the Net at the speed of light. But it doesn't actually go straight to the recipient's computer. It goes to the computer of their service provider and is held there for them until they download and read it.

So while an e-mail is *available* the instant you send it, it's not actually read until somebody checks their mail. Really urgent e-mails often get followed up by phone calls telling people to do just that.

But if e-mail is often slower than you'd think, it does have one huge advantage over all non-Internet forms of communication. It doesn't matter where you're sending – everything goes for the price of a local call. It doesn't matter whether you're writing to a friend in Australia or Japan or Outer Mongolia, you still pay only the local call rate.

E-mail doesn't confine you to text. You can send

photographs and drawings just as easily, along with software, speech, music and even mini-movies.

If your first Internet decision is to send some e-mail, you might also be interested in getting some back. If you don't want to rely on friends, you can subscribe to a mailing list.

Outside the Internet, *subscribe* means pay money. On the Net, it *can* mean pay money, but most of the time it just involves your leaving your e-mail address with a list manager. List managers aren't usually people. Mostly they're software that run the list and make sure that if your name's on it, you get all the e-mail generated by that list.

You will obviously only subscribe to a list that interests you. For example, if you subscribe to the *News of the Weird* mailing list (address *notw-request@nine.org*) you'll receive e-mail about things like weeping statues and exploding chickens.

There are lists devoted to just about any subject that might interest you.

The Internet

Site 14 — Illicit e-mail

►Despite the undoubted benefits of **e-mail** P.43, several companies have already discovered it has problems. The management of Eastman Kodak in New York ran an investigation into its e-mail system after discovering that employees had been using the convenient Net connection to post messages on **newsgroups** P.52.

The messages came complete with the company address so they looked like official Eastman Kodak communications. But the company itself knew nothing about them and had no control over what was in them.

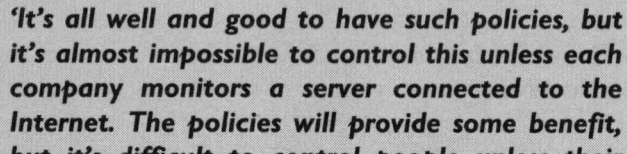

> *'It's all well and good to have such policies, but it's almost impossible to control this unless each company monitors a server connected to the Internet. The policies will provide some benefit, but it's difficult to control people unless their connection is turned off or their mail is forced to go through a clearing house.'*
> Robert Harvey, an analyst employed by the Internet Security Group.

Eastman Kodak weren't the only ones. The Wisconsin corporation Johnson Controls put in place a policy aimed at having some control over the way its employees use the Net. Their new policy forbade offensive or harassing statements on-line or sending out electronic chain letters. While they were at it, the management also denied their people the use of the Net to find another job.

Other companies have followed suit, including the Chase Manhattan and Amy Sudol banks.

> 'There will always be people misusing the Internet, but the majority will use it for knowledge.'
> Rosie, 15

THE INTERNET

Site 15 — World Wide Web

▶ The World Wide Web isn't so much a part of the Internet as a way of communicating with the Internet as a whole. You experience it as a series of electronic pages with hypertext links (just like this book) that stretches right across the Internet. The Web hasn't quite swallowed the entire Net yet, but it's well on the way — and for good reason. The World Wide Web is exciting.

It's also highly addictive.

The **browser**[P.39] you use to surf the Web will normally let you contact **newsgroups** [P.52] as well. It will also let you search for and download files. So for all practical purposes, once you get on to the Web, you won't ever need to get off it. Chances are you won't want to either.

> *The Writers Guild of America is poised to accept members who have written material for Web sites. You can earn as much as $25,000 as a Web author.*

Here's how it works.

Host computers on the Web store what's known as a Web page (or series of pages). You'll see why they're called pages the minute you link up with one. What appears on your screen is something like a page in a magazine or book.

Many of these pages are glossy, glamorous and chock-a-block with pictures and colour. Almost all contain text. Some have areas that play sounds or show brief movies if you click on them. There can be provision for you to send a message somewhere — usually back to the computer that stores the page you're looking at. In this way you can order goods from Web pages, join clubs from Web pages, or just tell somebody what you think of them from a Web page.

That's what makes the Web exciting. What makes it addictive is its links.

When you look at a Web page, you'll see that certain words or phrases are underlined, just like in this book. If you've got a colour monitor, you'll note they're also in blue. These words and phrases are known as hyperlinks. Click on them and you're transferred to another Web page that has more information. Some of the pictures act as hyperlinks as well – it doesn't have to be text.

> Only 10 per cent of those using the World Wide Web are over 40 years of age.

These transfers may be to Web pages on the same computer. But it's just as likely that they're stored on a different computer altogether ... and that computer may be on the far side of the world.

Every new Web page you reach will have its own underlined words and phrases, its own hyperlinks to other Web pages. And these pages will have hyperlinks to other pages. Once you're on-line to the Web, you can jump from one page to another, more or less indefinitely, following lines of information on the **topics that interest you** P.105.

You can find just about anything on the Internet, which means you can find just about anything on the Web. It's packed with libraries, art galleries, game sites, movie previews, shopping malls, on-line magazines and companies selling everything from videotapes to machines that put you into a trance.

> 'The variety of information you find is particularly distinctive, because the Web is a huge global network – one that allows countless students, professionals and knowledgeable people to share what they know. I love the fact that I have access to entire encyclopaedias and dictionaries.'
> Carolyn, 14

Each Web page is designated by its URL. The letters stand for Unique Resource Location, which is just a fancy way of describing an address. This is what a typical Web page URL address looks like:

http://www.vauxhall.co.uk/vectra

The letters *http* lets you know you're heading for a hypertext file.

The *www* means it's on the **World Wide Web** P.48.

Vauxhall.co is the Vauxhall Motor Company located in the United Kingdom (*uk*).

The last bit of the address tells you the page is devoted to the Vauxhall Vectra.

This address was published at the bottom of a double page colour spread in the *Sunday Times Magazine* in the hope you'd take notice and look at their Web page where you'd find a lot more information about the car.

But Web pages aren't just for commercial companies. Clubs, charitable organizations, churches, cults, political parties all have Web sites. So do ordinary people.

There's software available that lets you design your own Web page fairly easily. One package even claims that if you have 500 megabytes to spare on your hard disk, you can run it from your home.

WHAT YOU CAN DO ON THE NET

A rather more practical approach is to rent your own little bit of hyperspace from a service provider. Not all of them offer this service yet, but many do and the numbers are growing. A few will even offer you free gigabytes of space to set up your own Web pages as an incentive to join.

You can include anything you like in your own Web page. Your face can be seen by millions, your poetry read by millions, your opinions heard by millions. For the first time in history, you can save your pennies and buy fame.

> *'Nowadays, anybody can be famous for fifteen minutes.'* – pop artist Andy Warhol, 1928-87.

Not everything you'll find is nice   Site 38

THE INTERNET

Site 16 — Newsgroups

▶ When people find they can communicate with one another, it's human nature to form groups of similar interests. That's exactly what's happened on the Net. The groupings are called 'newsgroups'. The part of the Net that houses them is USENET.

Each newsgroup is a sort of electronic club set up for discussion of a particular topic.

They cover every subject you could imagine. From astronomy to flying saucers to chocolate. From cookery to ESP to mechanical engineering. From history to gossip to movies to music.

> *There are about 18,500 newsgroups already on the Net and more are being formed all the time.*

The browser **software** P.36 you use to link up with the **Web** P.48 will also (usually) let you contact Usenet newsgroups as well. In Netscape, you pull down the Window menu and select Netscape News. Explorer needs an add-on called *Mail and News* which is available free. If you're linked to the Net via CompuServe, the command GO USENET will take you there. If all else fails, go to a Web page that has software suited to your computer and download any newsreader package that appeals to you.

Despite the name newsgroup, you can forget your old definition of news. You can get news on the Internet – lots of it – but when you log on to a newsgroup, what you get is *opinion* and often *discussion*. There may be some real news in there, but it's largely accidental.

Essentially, Usenet is a collection of postings – some short notes, some lengthy articles – that are contributions to a discussion about a particular topic. What the topic is depends on the newsgroup where it was posted. Each newsgroup discusses one topic and one topic only. It might be making jam, brewing beer, eating turnips, Buddhism, Blur, cats, soccer or gardening.

To help you find your way around USENET, newsgroups have established a particular naming system that gives you an indication of what you're in for before you log on.

Each name is like a tree with its various branches separated by a full stop as in the following example:

rec.arts.marching.band.high-school

The first word *rec* represents the trunk of the tree and indicates the broad category into which the newsgroup falls. *Rec* stands for 'recreation' so you know already the group has something to do with amusement, relaxation, entertainment or that sort of thing. Other popular trunks are *alt* for 'alternative', *comp* for 'computer', *sci* for 'science', *soc* for 'sociology', *news* for matters related to the USENET newsgroups as a whole and *misc* for anything so weird it won't fit into the other categories.

The next word in the example is *arts* which tells you the newsgroup is into some sort of creative pursuit. The next word, *marching*, tells you what this is. When you come to *band* you discover what sort of marching the group is interested in and finally *high-school* narrows it down still further to let you know the focus is on high school marching bands.

You can check the content of this newsgroup for yourself. It actually exists.

The 18,500 current newsgroups service some 30 million users, so many of them are incredible sources of practical help and information. For example, if you positively must know the name of the fifth Beatle, find the relevant newsgroup and post your question. (Doing this is a lot like e-mail, although Usenet uses a different system.) Before you've had time to drink your Cola, the chances are you'll have your answer.

As well as questions and answers, newsgroups provide a forum for opinionated pronouncements on the things that interest you. Want people to read your new poem? Post it on the newsgroup:

rec.arts.poems.

Something to say about Arnie's latest movie? Then:
alt.fan.schwarzenegger,

(honestly!) wants to hear from you. And so it goes, from the newsgroup that deals with hangovers to the one that deals with virtual reality.

Some newsgroups are moderated. That's to say they have somebody screening stuff before it goes public. If you feel this is an invitation to censorship and that worries you, there's nothing to stop you taking your business elsewhere – there are endless newsgroups on the Net that aren't moderated at all.

But you never really appreciate the work of the moderator until you download the latest batch of messages from an unmoderated newsgroup. That's when you find some are repeated several times, some are corrupt files full of garble and some go over old ground.

> One of the most popular newsgroups on USENET is *alt.teens* which, you guessed it, discusses everything of interest to teenagers.

Some newsgroups get new postings at the rate of one or two a day. Others get them at the rate of one or two a *minute.* You can appreciate that even with modern computer storage capacity it's out of the question to keep

WHAT YOU CAN DO ON THE NET

every article and message indefinitely. Some newsgroups will hold material for as much as a week, but on average, postings are deleted after four days and a really popular group may have to delete more often.

If you want to contribute to this flood, it's a good idea to get yourself familiar with the rules of **netiquette** [P.63].

A few newsgroup addresses `Site 17` ▶
Trouble and how to avoid it `Site 20` ▶
Expressing your feelings `Site 21` ▶
Setting up your own group `Site 18` ▶

THE INTERNET

Site 17 — Useful newsgroups

▶ Newsgroups don't have pictures, **Java** P.60 applets or the various other bells and whistles of the **World Wide Web** P.48, but they are an information source that can be just as useful — in fact far more useful sometimes since you're less likely to be side-tracked.

Here are just a (very) few worth checking out:

alt.alien.research is a group devoted to a strictly unorthodox approach to the question of life — and intelligence — in Outer Space. If you want the latest buzz on UFOs (Unidentified Flying Objects), LGMs (Little Green Men), MIB (Men in Black) and other exciting X-File material, this is the place to gather.

alt.activism acknowledges the fact that from high school through university and (sometimes!) beyond, students take a great interest in changing the world around them. Although this group has a distinct US bias, the topics under discussion are fascinating, as are some of the suggested solutions to the world's problems. If you're interested in adding your tuppence-worth to discussions on, say, drug reform, this is the place to be.

alt.teens is exactly what it sounds like — a chance for teenagers to sound off on any subject of interest. And guess what? The No. 1 subject of interest for some years now has been sex!

soc.history can be a mine of information when you're running close to the deadline on your school project about the Life of Churchill, Ancient Rome, World War Two or Costumes in the Middle Ages. No matter how obscure the fact you need, there's bound to be somebody out there who has it and will answer your posting before you're due to hand your project in.

alt.algebra.help is plugged into a happy hinterland of friendly and obliging geniuses whose whole joy in life seems to be answering questions about algebra from those who find the subject about as comprehensible as Quantum Mechanics. Fantastic homework aid and if you ever get to like the subject, you'll find fun problems posted as well.

sci.math.research is a heavy-duty group for students who actually *do* find Quantum Mechanics — and similar obscure subjects — comprehensible. This one has discussions that sound to you and me like they're taking place on the far side of the moon. But while you won't need what's offered here every day, when you *do* need it you'll *really* need it.

◀ Site 16 **Newsgroup basics**
Setting up your own Site 18 ▶

Site 18 — Setting up your own

▶However many **newsgroups** P.52 there are, you may be interested in a topic so weird you can't find it discussed anywhere. If so, there's nothing to stop you launching your own.

There's a body of volunteers you can contact at:
group-mentors@acpub.duke.edu,

who are experienced in newsgroup creation. You don't *have* to contact them – the Internet is a lawless place – but it's a very good idea. They help people who want to form a new group. Give them an outline of your idea and somebody will help you submit a formal proposal.

> *You can get fuller advice on how to start your own newsgroup in Greg Woods' excellent article on* news.announce.newgroups

After certain preliminaries, the formation of the new group goes to a vote. To get that underway you contact the **USENET** P.52 Volunteer Votetakers (UVV) a neutral group who handle vote gathering and counting for all newsgroup proposals. The **e-mail** P.43 address of the group is:

uvv-contact@uvv.org.

This group then organizes a request for votes on the new group via the same newsgroups where you posted your original request for discussion. The voting period will last between 21 and 31 days after which the results will be announced, again through the same newsgroups.

There's a five day waiting period after the announcement, to give the Net a chance to correct any errors that may have occurred. After this the green light goes on if two-thirds of the votes received are in favour

What you can do on the Net

and there are at least a hundred more 'yes' votes than 'no' votes.

This process isn't backed by any law, but it's the way things are done on the Net, so if your newsgroup concept is bombed it's not a good idea to go ahead anyway even though, strictly speaking, there's nothing to stop you. If you're *really* keen to launch a group and you get turned down, you can always try again in six months.

◀ Site 16 Newsgroup basics

Site 19 — Netspeak

▶ One of the joys of surfing is you soon pick up a language nobody else understands. Not just slang like *netiquette* or *spam* but names and terms so specialized nobody hears them outside the Net.

Here are just a few need-to-knows:

Java

The subject of heady hype when it first appeared, Java is actually no more than one of the more recently developed programming languages like BASIC, PASCAL or C. But it does behave differently from most of them in that it creates mini applications, known as applets, which are automatically downloaded into your computer any time you visit a Java-enhanced site. Sounds pretty dull so far, but Java produces some neat animations and 3-D effects.

Since the software giant Microsoft decided to back Java as part of its development policy there's a very good chance that Java applets will become widespread on the Net. They may even become the standard way of producing neat effects ... at least until the next all-singing, all-dancing development comes along.

RealAudio

Progressive Networks developed the RealAudio sound format to meet one of the most common complaints voiced by teenage surfers. In the bad old days – and still in many parts of the Net today – the pleasure of visiting a **music site** P.188 quickly disappears when you have to wait half an hour or more for a download before you can listen to the music. RealAudio is a plug-in that puts a stop to that. Music (and other sound) files in this format start playing merrily a few seconds after you begin the download.

What you can do on the Net

Shockwave
This is a graphics-handling tool developed by Macromedia that has taken quite a few Web page designers by storm, largely because it's very good at animation.

GIFs
If you come across a file labelled GIF anywhere on the Net, you know you're dealing with pictures. The letters stand for Graphic Interchange Format, a standard devised to allow the downloading of graphics across a wide variety of different computers. Early GIFs were stills, black and white or colour, but the 89a version of the format allows for simple animations.

JPEG
Picture files can grow large, especially where they involve high detail and full colour, so downloading them into your computer could cause a very real time problem. JPEG was one of the earliest solutions, a compression format specially designed for pictorial material. When a file is labelled JPEG, you're dealing with a compressed picture. It will download fast – or at least a lot faster than it would if it wasn't compressed – but you'll need special software to look at it. JPEGView, widely available on the Net, does the job very nicely and at 750K doesn't take up too much space on disk.

FAQ
Stands for Frequently Asked Questions and usually indicates a text file dealing with the subject you're investigating. Since FAQ files are, almost by definition, aimed at presenting the most basic information about the subject (in easy-to-follow question and answer form) they're a great place for Internet beginners to start. Run a

search on the thing that interests you, then access any FAQ files indicated on the site.

What you can do on the Net

Site 20 — Netiquette

▶The Internet is about interaction. First-time users take a while just surfing and absorbing the truth – or otherwise – that's out there. But sooner or later, the temptation to participate gets just too much. When it happens to you, you'll need to know the rules of netiquette.

> *'When thou enter a city, abide by its customs.'* — this quote from the Talmud heads the Netiquette WWW page at www.primenet.com/~vez/neti.html

There's no **law on the Internet** P.130. But there are customs. Break too many of them and your fellow surfers will find some way to make your life a misery. The most popular method is **flaming** P.97.

First rule of netiquette is don't evangelize. The ideal of the Internet is free speech, but that shouldn't be taken as licence to force your opinions down somebody's throat.

The next is that you keep to the subject. If the subject under discussion is pet rabbits, you're not entitled to post an article about Kylie Minogue, however interesting it might be. (Unless, of course, you've discovered some incredible secret link between Kylie and pet rabbits.)

It's a good idea to read existing postings before you start contributing your own. That way you avoid going over old ground – another breach of netiquette – and get an idea how things work in the particular **newsgroup** P.52.

> *'In the entire history of the Net, no one has managed to do this without looking like a complete idiot.'* – Internet comment on evangelism.

Next, forget about posting articles that are all in CAPITAL LETTERS. This really drives people demented, partly because it's tiring to read, but mainly because in a **newsgroup** P.52 it's held to be the universal sign of ignorance at best and sheer rudeness at worst.

The only time you can get away with capitals is if you're emphasizing a point. Even then, it's better to use asterisks for emphasis. You put them *before* and *after* the words you want to emphasize.

Keep your message plain. Avoid jargon, mysterious abbreviations, initials nobody understands and waffle. Keep your signature plain as well. If you've nothing better to do, you'll find it's possible to make all sorts of spectacular pictures out of text. Having found it out, forget it. Some idiots use these pictures to embellish their signatures. If you join them, you're in breach of netiquette.

Make sure the material you're posting is your own. Or, if you really want to pass on something written by somebody else, make sure you have their permission and, again with their permission, credit them with it.

> *'We Americans have made fools of ourselves by forgetting [other countries have their own values] everywhere else. Let's try to behave a little better on the Net.'* – posted comment on netiquette.

Finally, here's a list of more technical do's and don'ts culled from posted advice on netiquette:

☐ **Don't** include the entire contents of a previous posting in your reply. You may find the software you're using does this automatically. If so, override it.

☐ **Do** leave just enough to show what you're responding to. Remember to include who said it since there may be a number of postings between the original message and your reply.

☐ **Don't** send irritating messages demanding who wants to talk about the subject under discussion or asking why nobody's dealing with some other subject that interests you.

☐ **Do** separate your paragraphs with blank lines. This makes your message more readable.

☐ **Don't** send lines longer than 70 characters. Some of your readers will have terminal-based mail editors or newsreaders that can't handle any more.

☐ **Do** remember nobody can hear your tone of voice. This is something that makes sarcasm, satire and humour particularly difficult to post. Use **emoticons** P.66 to give clues to your emphasis.

Site 21 — Emoticons

▶ Emoticons are a Net invention that came about because while you can talk to just about anybody over the Net, you can't see their face.

If you tell a friend face to face that she smells like an orangutan's armpit, she can see from your expression you don't really mean it.

But if she can't see your expression, she might reach for the deodorant ... or the nearest blunt instrument.

To avoid this sort of hassle, Net surfers have developed a whole series of facial expressions that can actually be sent as part of the message text.

Here are some of the good ones. If they don't make sense to you at first, try holding the page sideways when you look at them.

:-)	I'm smiling
:-(	I'm frowning
:-|)	I'm laughing
:'-(	I'm crying
;—)	I'm winking
:-o	I'm shocked
:-p	I'm sticking out my tongue
:-L—	I'm drooling

What you can do on the Net

If you want to be really nice to somebody, you can send them a single long-stemmed red rose:

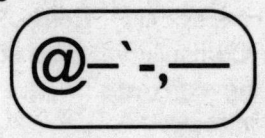

@--`-,—

Or, if they're a trekkie, you can give them Spock's Vulcan salute:

\\//

Live long and prosper, baby, \o/. (That last sign means Hallelujah.)

There are also several acronyms in common usage:

GRD   Grinning, running and ducking

NRN   No reply necessary

OTOH   On the other hand

ROTFL   Rolling on the floor laughing

GAL   Get a life

IMHO   In my humble opinion

And so on, including a great many that can't be included here because they're rude. Now you know them, remember not to overuse them unless you want to risk being <u>**flamed**</u> P.97.

THE INTERNET

Site 22 — Chat

▶Commercial services like CompuServe pioneered electronic chat. In CompuServe, chat sites are known as *forums*, which, like **newsgroups** P.52, are dedicated to the discussion of specific topics.

Typically a forum has a message board where you can leave notes for other members, a library, where you can download files on the topic of interest, and a meeting room where you can communicate directly with any other member who happens to be on line at the time.

But you no longer need to subscribe to a commercial service in order to talk to fellow surfers. The rest of the Internet has caught up in a big way thanks to something known as IRC.

IRC stands for Internet Relay Chat, a system that lets you communicate with your fellow surfers *in real time*. You type in what you want to say at your computer keyboard. Your words appear immediately on the other screens and the people you're talking to can respond at once.

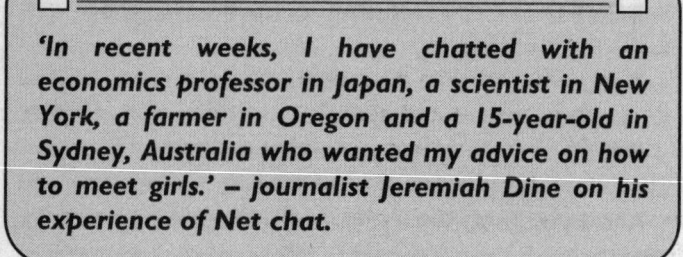

> 'In recent weeks, I have chatted with an economics professor in Japan, a scientist in New York, a farmer in Oregon and a 15-year-old in Sydney, Australia who wanted my advice on how to meet girls.' – journalist Jeremiah Dine on his experience of Net chat.

To get involved in chat, the first thing you need to do is check out the **World Wide Web** P.48 pages of the subnets where the chat takes place. These are currently

What you can do on the Net

the biggest:
 DALnet (*www.dal.net*),
 Efnet (*irc.ucdavis.edu/efnet/*) and,
 Undernet (*www.undernet.org*).

The DALnet page will tell you where to download the necessary software, known as a client program. The most popular packages seem to be mIRC for use with PCs and Ircle for the Macintosh.

All three sites will direct you to servers handling chat, although most of the software you download will have one or two connections built in. For those that don't, start-up preferences will normally allow you to specify which IRC server of the nearly 200 available to connect. You'll need to type in the name of the server and sometimes its port number. That second bit sounds tricky, but you'll almost certainly get away with typing in 6667, which is the default port number of most of them. If this doesn't work, try leaving out the number altogether.

Communication on IRC is done by way of channels and private messages. You'll recognize a channel by the fact that its name starts with the symbol # denoting a public channel or & which shows it's a local channel. There are thousands of channels to choose from, but check out *TeenChat* and *Luv2Flirt*.

As soon as you join a channel, everything you type is sent to that channel and seen by all other users on that channel. You, in turn, can see what anybody else types. You can send or receive private messages which can't be seen by anybody on the channel other than the person it's directed to.

The most useful IRC commands are:

/HELP gets you more info on how things work.

/JOIN followed by the name of the channel lets you join that channel.

/LIST shows you all the channels available on the server.

/ME followed by the text you type sends a description of what you're doing in the third person.

/MSG sends a private message.

/WHO IS followed by a nickname brings you all the information a user has entered about himself/herself.

An interesting aspect of IRC, is that you're identified only by a nickname – and you get to pick that nickname yourself. Nicknames can't be more nine characters long, except on DALnet which allows longer names. You'll also typically be asked to register some information about yourself, but not much and nobody checks that you aren't making it up.

The popularity of Internet chat persuaded the Time-Warner Corporation to establish a more sophisticated chat service on the Net called The Palace.

Like ordinary IRC, you have to set yourself up with the necessary software and find a server that plays host to Palace chatting. Visit the Palace Home Page on the Web at:
http://www.thepalace.com
for instructions on how to find both.

But when you run the software you'll find yourself involved in something very different to simple lines of type.

> *There is software available that lets you create your own Palace on your own computer and open it up to others on the Net. Once you've created the necessary graphics, you can build a 20-room Palace in about an hour.*

First, in place of the usual IRC nickname, you can build yourself a visible personality (known as an 'avatar') using imported photographs or graphics, or selected from a variety of 'props' available on the Palace site. The avatar you create is what other users see when you enter the Palace environment.

The Palace is a step towards virtual reality because when you log on you find yourself in a building with various different rooms. You can travel from room to room, examining the various things you find there, playing games, changing stuff around, even leaving new items for others to find.

But the big thing about the Palace is that you can see, talk to and interact with the avatars of other on-line users who happen to be present at the same time you are.

If the whole business of setting yourself up with IRC software seems just too much trouble, you can still engage in real-time chat via the **World Wide Web** P.48. Point your browser to:

http://www.yahoo.com/Computers_and_Internet/Internet/Chatting/
for comprehensive information on the sites available.

Why you should be careful out there `Site 40` ▶
◀ `Site 20` **The Information Super Highway Code**

Section Five
IS THE NET A MURDEROUS MONSTER?

THE INTERNET

IS THE NET A MURDEROUS MONSTER?

Site 23 — The first 'Internet'

▶ During the fifteenth century a new piece of world-changing technology appeared that had very similar effects to the Internet today. The technology was the printing press and it was able to spread knowledge far more quickly and far more widely than knowledge had ever been spread before ... just like the Internet.

Books existed before the printing press, of course, but they had to be copied or block printed laboriously by hand. That's a slow and costly process. A run-away bestseller might warrant an edition of, say, fifty copies.

Of course the printing press didn't just spread knowledge. It wasn't long before people realized it could be used to spread entertainment as well ... just like the Internet.

The earliest narrative prose fiction was probably written by the Greek Aristides in the Second Century BC. But the first novel as we know it today was a work called *Pamela* by Samuel Richardson published in 1740.

Pamela had a sub-title, *Virtue Rewarded*, to make sure potential purchasers knew what they were getting. And potential purchasers, reading between the lines, knew they were getting something to do with sex.

Before long, a hefty proportion of the output of the printing press was devoted to pornography ... just like the Internet.

Porn on the Net Site 38 ▶
History of the Internet Site 28 ▶

THE INTERNET

Site 24 — Luddites

▶ In the 1760s, technology took a great leap forward when James Watt and John Wilkinson dramatically improved the design of the steam engine. Soon steam power was driving a wide range of factory and mill machinery. The world had an industrial revolution on its hands.

Not everybody liked it. English workers known as Luddites started a campaign of smashing industrial machinery.

The Luddite movement began in the lace industries around Nottingham in 1811 and spread to the wool and cotton mills of Yorkshire and Lancashire. An unsympathetic government put paid to the whole sorry business by hanging 14 Luddites in York.

All the same, it was the first clear sign of widespread public concern about technology.

Today, the Luddites are usually dismissed as nutters standing in the way of progress. But while their worry at the time was losing jobs, they seem to have figured out something we should all think about – technology doesn't *always* build a better world.

The technology of the Internet is just as revolutionary as the steam engine. It carries the potential for even more change. It is appealing to the point of **addiction** P.157.

Is there anybody today asking seriously whether it will build a better world?

Technologies that didn't build a better world Site 26 ▶

IS THE NET A MURDEROUS MONSTER?

Site 25 — Frankenstein technology

▶Mary Shelley's classic horror tale tells how scientist Baron Victor Von Frankenstein tried to create life by joining together parts of different corpses and animating the result with electricity.

The monster escaped from his control, wreaked havoc in the world and eventually killed its master.

According to psychologists, the story became popular because it tapped into humanity's *Frankenstein complex*, a deep-seated fear of creating something that gets out of control. Historians sometimes refer to *Frankenstein technology*, referring to inventions like the H-bomb (and even the computer) which they believe may one day destroy the humanity that made them.

Frankenstein technology typically follows three stages. The first is the stage of innocent development. The designers do not necessarily realize the thing they're working on may be dangerous. The second is when the technology gets out of control. The third is when it becomes lethal.

If you study **how the Internet began** P.85 one thing quickly becomes very clear. At an early stage of its development, the network started to run out of control. The original ARPAnet was named after America's Advanced Research Projects Agency, which is a branch of the Pentagon. The Pentagon, in turn, is the American military control centre.

There is no doubt at all that the network came into being to give generals something else to play with. But almost from the very start, it slipped its leash and ran free from military control.

By 1983, the military themselves admitted this when they established the sub-network, MILNET, which was under their control. Meanwhile, the rest of the Net kept growing and became more lawless with each passing year. The process continues to this day.

There is no question at all that the Internet has passed the second stage so typical of Frankenstein Technology. It is well and truly out of control.

The question now is whether it will turn around and bite us.

Site 26 — Technology that turned

▶ In 1872, something called the Solvay process revolutionized the chemical industry and set it on the road to a growth which polluted rivers on almost every continent.

The petroleum industry was born in 1859, when Edwin L. Drake sank an oil well in the USA. During the nineteenth century it produced mainly kerosene for people's lamps, but then in 1913 Henry Ford started to mass produce automobiles.

Between them, these two pieces of technology — oil extraction and automobile manufacturing — have depleted the world's natural resources, contributed to air pollution and buried thousands of acres of land under tarmac and concrete.

When the Wright Brothers put wings on a bicycle in 1903, they believed they were fulfilling man's ancient desire to fly. By 1945, aeroplanes were a dominant feature of warfare.

Plastics looked like a real boon when they were first introduced. We only discovered their downside when we tried to throw them away. They take for ever to biodegrade.

Chemical fertilizers and pesticides were good news when they were developed. Then farmers found many of the former ruined the land while many of the latter poisoned the crops.

Antibiotics were first widely used during the Second World War. They saved millions of lives and continue to save millions of lives to this day. They have also begun to breed superbugs which experts are predicting will become the Black Death of the twenty-first century.

More ingenious developments in weapons technology

have included long-range artillery, machine guns, poison gas, torpedoes, tanks, ballistic missiles and, above all, the atomic bomb.

Not content with that last little horror, humanity took no more than a decade to develop fusion weapons which could literally wipe out all life on the planet.

Is the Net a murderous monster?

Site 27 — Electronic democracy?

▶ Fans of the Internet frequently describe it as a global democracy, a worldwide source of information and entertainment that will revolutionize life on our planet. The reality falls short of the hype.

In 1996, China opened its doors to the Internet ... and closed them again only a few months later. The authorities in the country that houses a quarter of the world's population just did not like the freedom of information the Net brought to its citizens.

Should you live in any one of several other dictatorships – notably the more repressive regimes of Asia and the Middle East – you can be shot nowadays for watching satellite TV.

Most people believe what they're watching on television news is real, that the pictures on the screen show actual events. But news – even television news – may be slanted to manipulate opinion. It can even be faked entirely. Given a ruthless enough government, there's no reason why special effects can't be applied to news pictures. It certainly has been in the past. At least one Soviet leader – Leonid Brezhnev – was still appearing on television after his death because it didn't suit the Kremlin to admit he'd gone.

When you're running a dictatorship, propaganda is important. You need it to keep your people in line and, hopefully, control what they think. Successful action is only as good as the information it's based on. If you control the information, you control the action.

In this context, the Internet poses a far greater threat to the world's dictatorships than any previous technical development – including satellite TV. Once your people are wired into the Net, you can no longer control the information available to them. Which means you can no longer expect them to believe your propaganda. Since most dictatorships (and quite a few democracies) keep their people in line by telling them lies, you can see how the Internet becomes a threat. If you're a dictator, your first instinct must be to ban it ... which, after their brief flirtation, is exactly what the Chinese did.

Supporters of the Internet stress its potential in raising the standard of living in the Third World. In the developed world, business people have taken to the Net in a big way. It cuts costs and makes their companies more efficient. Pretty soon, a business that isn't wired simply won't be able to compete. If you add together the various businesses in a country you've got an economy. Countries whose economies aren't wired won't be able to compete either. Those that are will do far better.

But the idea that the Net represents some sort of salvation for the Third World is naïve. The Internet is an information source confined to an elite with enough money to buy a home computer and a modem, enough money to have a telephone installed, enough to pay their electricity bill, **service provider** P.33 charges, phone bills.

And this does not even describe the majority of the population of the developed world. When you stop to consider the teeming millions in rural Africa and Asia, millions who cannot afford to buy a potato let alone a computer, the idea that we have created a wholly democratic electronic communications web around our planet is downright laughable.

And many think this is just one area in which the Internet is a lot less significant than it appears to be.

Hassles with the Net (1) Site 37 ▶
Hassles with the Net (2) Site 38 ▶
Hassles with the Net (3) Site 47 ▶

Section Six

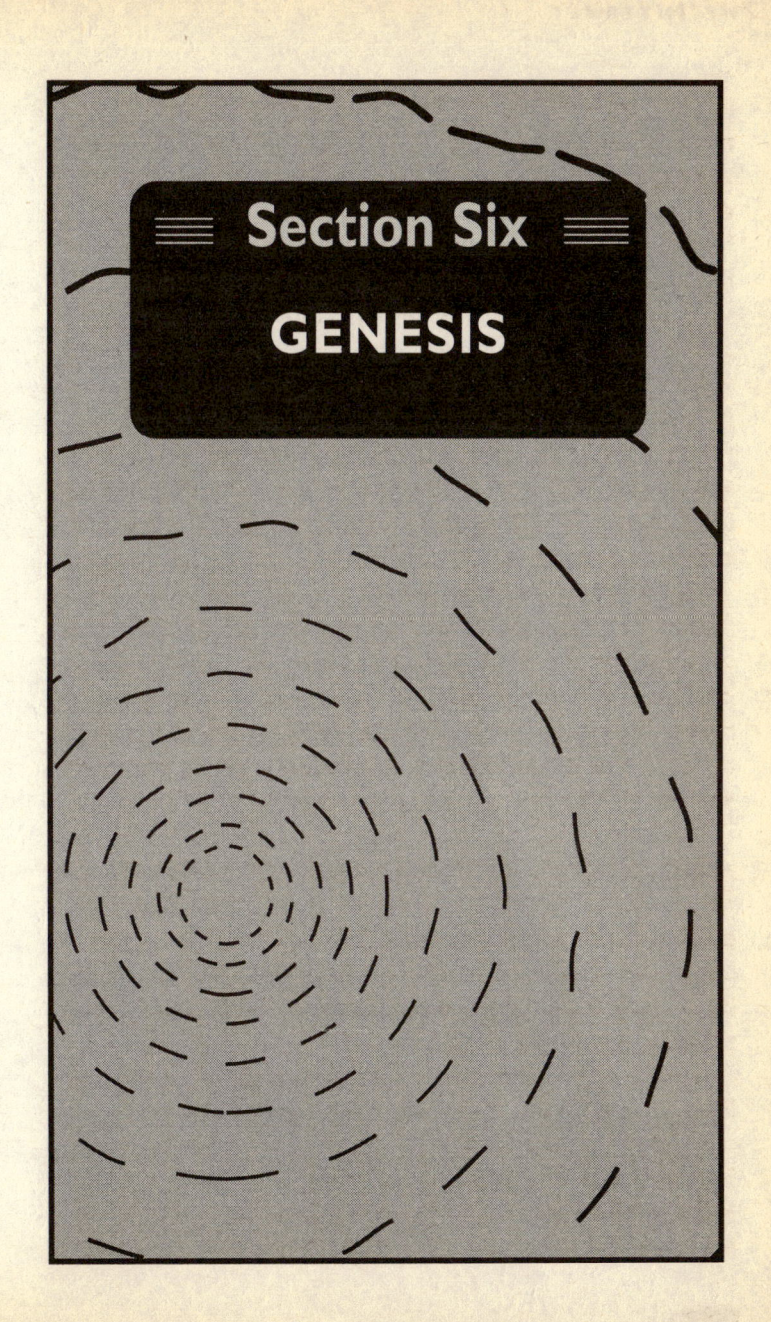

GENESIS

GENESIS

Site 28 — How it started

▶ Back in the 1960s, two world superpowers, the United States and the Soviet Union were engaged in something called a Cold War.

The Cold War consisted of threats, propaganda, political manoeuvring, lies, insults, spying, double-dealing, treachery, non-cooperation and, occasionally, economic sanctions. What it didn't involve was shooting – because both superpowers were afraid of what might happen to the world if a war went nuclear – which explains why it was called a 'cold' war.

But both sides invested a lot of time and energy trying to figure out ways of surviving a nuclear war ... just in case.

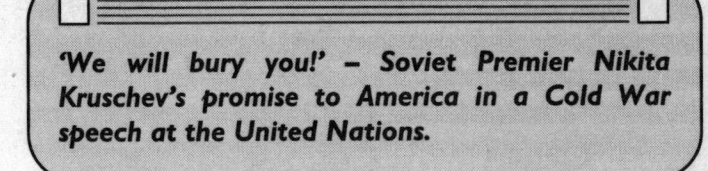

'We will bury you!' – Soviet Premier Nikita Kruschev's promise to America in a Cold War speech at the United Nations.

One of the big problems was how to keep things going after a nuclear strike. Good communications were obviously needed – especially secret and secure links between military bases. Also needed were phone links between cities that could be used by commerce and industry and finance.

All these links form a network that's taken for granted in peacetime. Unfortunately it's a network that would never survive a nuclear strike.

In fact, when the American leadership started to think about it in the 1960s, it occurred to them that *no network they could imagine* would survive a nuclear strike. You

The Internet

couldn't build a nuclear shelter round every piece of switching gear or every metre of wire. The minute the bombs started falling, your communications system would be in chaos.

There was another problem. How did you keep control? Any control headquarters, however secret, would eventually become known to the enemy. And once they found where it was, they'd bomb it.

The American military passed the dilemma on to the Rand Corporation of Santa Monica, California, which specializes in problem solving. An employee, Paul Baran, cracked it.

Rand published Baran's proposals in 1964. They answered the two big questions in a wholly unexpected way.

> ☐ **Question:** How do you stop your control headquarters from being wiped out in a nuclear attack?
>
> ☐ **Answer:** You don't have a control headquarters.
>
> ☐ **Question:** How do you cope with a communications network that's in bits when the bombs start falling?
>
> ☐ **Answer:** You build a network that's designed to work when it's in bits.

A node is a junction where several lines of a system come together. Baran's idea was that every node in his proposed network would be equal to the old-style central control headquarters. It would be able to send messages, to receive messages, to pass on messages.

Baran's next idea was that you didn't send a continuous data stream the way it had been done up to then. The messages would be converted into electronic packets. These packets worked the same way as a letter in the mail. They were marked with an address.

But Baran decided the packet didn't have to go straight there. It could take any route it liked. All that mattered was that it got there.

Baran figured that if somebody bombed the network, it wouldn't matter. The packets simply went around the devastated areas and got through eventually. Since they moved with the speed of an electrical pulse, they weren't even slowed down.

In 1968, the National Physical Laboratory in the UK set up a small experimental network to see if these ideas would work in practice.

They did. And that got the military interested.

In America, the military decided to pour money into a bigger, better network. By Christmas, 1969, they had the start of a network up and running. It was pretty small. There were only four nodes. But each node was a supercomputer costing hundreds of thousands of dollars and capable of working what looked like computer miracles in those days.

In this tiny network lay the deep roots of what would eventually become the Internet.

Those four computers were connected by lines that weren't used for anything else. They could send information to each other and if you were sitting at one, you could program any of the others.

The system was called ARPAnet.

In the bright new year of 1971, the number of nodes in ARPAnet jumped from four to fifteen. The following year it had more than doubled to a total of thirty-seven.

It wasn't just the military who were using ARPAnet. The military certainly provided the funding, but right from the start this little network was used by colleges and scientists as well.

In fact, since there wasn't a war on, the schools and scientists were using the network *more* than the military. And they weren't using it the way the military had planned.

At the start, the men behind ARPAnet thought the big benefit would be long-distance computing – sitting at one terminal and using another computer somewhere else. But the way the network was actually being used was very different.

Researchers were sending *information* back and forth. They were getting together on projects. Worse still, they were sending personal messages.

In other words, they were using the network for **electronic mail** P.43 and the Government was paying.

Around about this time, somebody invented the electronic mailing list. This was a system by which one message could be sent to a whole long list of receivers at the same time.

To the horror of those who thought they were **in charge** P.92, it wasn't sober, sensible messages that were being sent. Most of them were discussing science fiction.

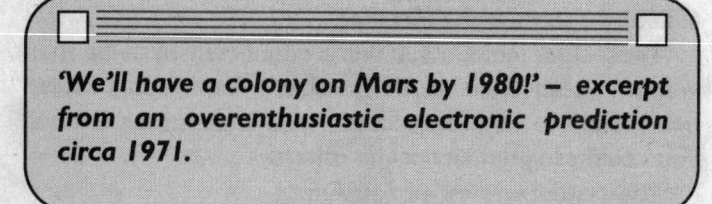

'We'll have a colony on Mars by 1980!' – *excerpt from an overenthusiastic electronic prediction circa 1971.*

Official disapproval made no difference. The people on ARPAnet kept sending silly messages to one another. And the system kept growing.

ARPAnet was designed to accept any type of **computer** P.27. It didn't matter whether you were using an IBM or a DEC or any one of the dozens of other machines coming on to the market. If it had the capability and the software to deal with information packets, it could come aboard.

After ARPAnet had been running for a year or two, the way it dealt with information packets was changed. A new **protocol** P.35 was introduced. It was so sophisticated it allowed other networks to join ARPAnet, even if their ways of doing things were different. By 1977, other networks were indeed joining in.

In 1983, the military, who were nominally in control of ARPAnet all this time, got tired of trying to nursemaid a bunch of unruly nerds who used the Net to gossip. So they set up their own specialized network, MILNET.

But it was far too late to start a whole new ball game. MILNET was linked into ARPAnet, which itself was almost unrecognizable since it was now linked into a whole host of other little networks and single computers which had very little to do with anything military and nothing at all to do with war.

Anybody could get the **protocol** P.35 software. They didn't even have to pay. So if you had your own computer network or even just your own computer, you could join in with no problem at all. Since there was no control headquarters, there was nobody to stop you.

The bigger ARPAnet grew the more useful it was to everybody on it.

> *'When growth is not properly regulated, anomalies and tumours may result.'* – Encyclopaedia Britannica.

Independent networks with names like BITNET, USENET and UUCP all joined in. From 1984 throughout the remainder of the decade, the National Science Foundation built five supercomputer centres to give any academic researcher access to high-power computers formerly available only to military contractors.

Then they built their own network to connect the five regional centres together.

Then they got the existing university networks to chain together and link to the closest NSFNET regional centre.

Then, since everybody was using the same protocol software, they linked with the by now enormous ARPAnet.

Except it was silly to call it ARPAnet any more. ARPAnet, like all the other nets, was just one small piece of an expanding supernet that was way above and beyond any one of them.

NASA jumped in. So did the US Department of Energy, the Health Authorities and heaven knows who else. Computer networking was growing like crazy. In 1989, ARPAnet formally ceased to exist.

Most of its users didn't even notice.

Around this time something else was going on that was to have an explosive impact on the growth of the worldwide computer network. The Soviet Union was in trouble. By 1991, it was falling apart. In December of that year, the leaders of Russia, Ukraine and Belarus declared that a Commonwealth of Independent States would replace the old Union of Soviet Socialist Republics.

The Cold War was over.

While the Cold War was still on, there was some attempt by the authorities to keep control of the network. For example, university scientists were warned about storing their notes on the system since the Soviets were routinely tapping in and reading them.

But with the Cold War finished, there was nothing to stop the network going public. And the public was more than ready. The savings to be gained from **e-mail** P.43 alone were enough to convince many businesses – and even private people – to invest in the equipment needed for connection.

By the early 1990s, the international computer web we now know as the Internet was well and truly up and running.

THE INTERNET

Site 29 — Who's in control?

➤ There's a published article about the Net that ends with these words: 'The Internet is overseen by The Internet Society, a loosely affiliated group of individual and corporate volunteers with offices in Reston, Va.' This gives the impression there's somebody out in Reston running the show.

There isn't.

The Internet Society is a non-profit-making organization with four broad aims:

1 To help the technical development of the Net as an instrument for research and education. To do this, the Society tries to encourage academic, scientific and engineering organizations to climb aboard. Most of them don't need much persuading.

2 To educate everybody about how the Net works and how to use it.

3 To push the scientific and educational applications of the Net which they feel will benefit people.

4 To encourage discussion and development of new ways the Internet can be used and to persuade various organizations to get together to do so. But it's not in charge.

GENESIS

> *'The Internet Society does not operate the Internet. Internet operation continues to be a collaborative activity which the Society seeks to facilitate. The Society provides assistance and support to groups and organizations involved in the use, operation and evolution of the Internet.'* – quote from a policy document issued by The Internet Society.

The Internet Activities Board has been in operation since 1983. It's been reorganized several times and now has two main parts: the Internet Engineering Task Force and the Internet Research Task Force.

The Internet Engineering Task Force looks after existing **protocols** P.35 while the Internet Research Task Force tries to develop better ones. A bit like the Internet Society, the Internet Activities Board publishes documents that describe the Net and specify the technical specs for its operation.

They don't run things either.

> *The only person who comes close to running the show is Kibo (alias James Parry of Massachusetts) who has been threatening via his newsgroup alt.religion.kibology to close down all existing newsgroups and replace them with three new hierarchies – nonbozo*, bozo* and megabozo*. It may be significant that he makes these threats annually ... on 1 April.*

93

The Internet Assigned Numbers Authority and the Internet Registry are central stores for Internet information and give out new names to the various networks that are coming on board.

The Internet Registry also looks after the Domain Name System database used to make sure the electronic mail runs smoothly.

If you want to set up a new domain, you need to apply to these people, but that's only so you don't call your domain by the same name as one already in the Net and confuse people.

Beyond that, they're not telling you what to do.

Finally there's a Co-ordinating Committee for Intercontinental Networks organized by the US Federal Networking Council and a European *Réseaux Associées pour la Recherche Européenne* which both help co-ordinate plans for government-sponsored research networking.

They don't tell you what to do either.

The simple answer to the simple question of who's in charge round here is ... nobody.

So how, in theory, does it keep from chaos? Site 30 ▶

And in practice? Site 31 ▶

Site 30 — Net customs

➤ Although there's no law enforcement, let alone any law, on the Net, there are customs that have grown up out of the group soul of the Net.

You abuse them at your peril.

It's a bit like the Old West without the guns and a bit like a science fiction story published some years ago.

In this story you had a society where everybody was eligible to become supreme dictator. You just put your name on a list and when it reached the top, you got to run the country.

There was absolutely no limit to your power. You could do anything you wanted to anybody you wanted. You were above the law and answerable to nobody. But when you got the job, there was a small charge of explosive surgically implanted at the base of your skull. This charge was wired to a radio-controlled detonator.

All around the country were things like phone booths, except that inside them was a single big red button. Anybody could go into these booths at any time and press the button if they disagreed with your policies.

Each press of the button sent a radio signal to a computer linked to the detonator in your skull. When the number of signals went above a certain level, it triggered the charge and blew your head off.

That's more or less the way it works on the Net. It's been called the first real example of **direct democracy** P.81 in human history because there's no elected government, no ruling council, no military dictator and the only rules and regulations are those agreed by the participants themselves.

But as you'll see in **Flame wars** P.97 you can still come

close to getting your head blown off.

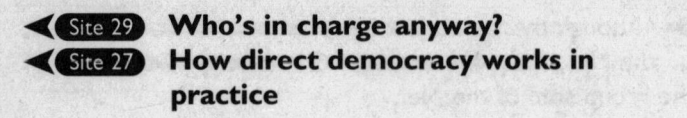

◀ Site 29 **Who's in charge anyway?**
◀ Site 27 **How direct democracy works in practice**

Site 31 — Flame wars

▶A few years ago, an American company named Canter and Siegal decided **newsgroups** P.52 were the perfect place to advertise. Compared to Press and other media advertising, reaching the millions who subscribed to newsgroups cost next to nothing. They posted ads to just about every newsgroup on the Net. It wasn't against the law. There was nobody in charge to tell them not to.

But all the same the roof fell in.

What the company did is technically known as *spamming* and Internet users didn't like it. They reacted in their thousands. The result was a flame war.

Flaming means sending somebody abusive material — usually very abusive material. A flame war means there's a lot of it flying about. Mail bombs are text files, either empty or full of random rubbish, designed to clutter up the recipient's electronic mailbox.

You can imagine what it must have been like. The corporation execs come in bright and early on the day after their exercise in mega-spamming. They check their **e-mail** P.43 for replies to their ad. The mailbox is full! It's packed to capacity. There are so many replies the company is going to be booked up until the year 3000.

Except when they start to download, they find most of those replies are empty files or garbage and those that aren't are telling them where to stick their spam. And this goes on all day. Because you have to check each incoming bit of mail just in case it might be a genuine response.

> 'Back in the good old days of USENET, spammers would be blasted from the Net with mail bombs ... but spams are so common now that there's not a huge amount you can do apart from keep adding the senders' e-mail addresses to your ever-burgeoning kill file.' – advice given to a reader of .net magazine in 1996 when he complained of the amount of spam he was finding in his electronic mailbox.

In fact it didn't just go on all day – it went on for days on end, tying up corporation computer time and corporation executive time. The volume of hate mail grew so enormous that the **service provider** P.33 which acted as the corporation's gateway to the Net found it couldn't cope. They did the only thing possible. They cut the link.

That was the most dramatic example (yet) of what happens when you break the rules of netiquette. It's left most commercial corporations very wary about spamming. But you can find yourself flamed – or, less often, mail bombed – for a lot less. Try expressing a really rudely unpopular opinion, for example. Like 'Everybody who believes in flying saucers is a CRETIN' on *alt.news.ufo*, for example.

Tips posted on the Net for avoiding a flame war include:

> ☐ Be diplomatic in the way you express your opinions. Remember that while something works for you, it may not appeal to others ... and they have an absolute right to go their own way and even make their own mistakes.

☐ Apologize when necessary – and even when it isn't. It's probably true to say a majority of hassles arise from misunderstanding. Take responsibility for being unclear in what you said (even if you weren't), apologize and try to put the point again more clearly.

☐ Avoid flame bait. That's to say, don't engage in conduct you know is likely to run contrary to the morals and customs of a particular group. Take time to find out how a newsgroup operates and the sort of discussion that goes on within it *before* you start posting messages of your own. The beginning of a school term is a good time to do this. That's when a good many newbies climb on board the interesting newsgroups. Watch what happens to them and learn by their mistakes.

☐ Learn where the power lies and avoid head to head confrontation. Every newsgroup has long-standing members who've earned the respect of the group. They've reached their present position through knowledge and long service. By becoming abusive to one of these individuals, you'll not only make an enemy of him or her, but you'll also upset a wide circle of their friends – which may include everybody in the group but you!

◀ Site 13   **For the basics on e-mail**
◀ Site 16   **For the basics on newsgroups**

Section Seven
THINGS YOU CAN FIND ON THE NET

Site 32 — Fishing with the Net

▶The Internet is often called the Information Superhighway and hyped as the ultimate source of universally accessible data on the planet. But is it?

There's no argument about the **quantity of information** P.20 now stored on the Net. It is the library to end all libraries, the reference source that tops all reference sources. Anything you could ever want to know about is there.

The trouble is finding it.

A *Guardian* journalist wrote how he spent several hours on the Internet searching for information he later found within five minutes in the local library.

His experience is by no means unique. Most people coming on to the Net quickly discover all that wonderful information could be anywhere – and most of it is buried under the world's biggest heap of electronic rubbish.

Even when you do locate what you are looking for, your troubles are far from over. The Internet is unregulated. Anyone can post anything on it, and the information doesn't have to be accurate – or even true.

There's an ancient Roman warning that should appear on every computer screen before an Internet download – *caveat emptor*, 'let the buyer beware', even though the buyer in this case isn't paying anything.

It's human nature to give weight to something that appears in print – one reason for the frequently repeated warning not to believe everything you read in the papers. If this is true for print media, which usually has some sort of reputation to protect, it is doubly true for the Internet whose only reputation is that of a free-for-all.

> *'All of the expressions once contained in books or film strips or records or newsletters will exist either as pure thought or something very much like thought: voltage conditions darting around the Net at the speed of light, in conditions that one might behold in effect, as glowing pixels or transmitted sounds, but never touch or claim to "own" in the old sense of the word.'* – John Perry Barlow

Your real protection is to realize that while the Internet as a whole is utterly unreliable, many sites within it are not. You can, for example, subscribe to the *Encyclopaedia Britannica* and many other reputable reference sources via the Net and the information you download from such sites is just as reliable as in a book.

The same goes for the many newspapers that have now gone on-line. If you trust their printed pages, you can trust their electronic editions as well.

But where the information you fish from the Net comes from a source unknown to you, treat it with caution. Cross check – something always possible on the Net – or consult an expert in the field.

For help on finding things on the Net　Site 33 ▶

THINGS YOU CAN FIND ON THE NET

Site 33 — Finding what you want

▶The *Guardian* journalist mentioned in Site 32 almost certainly had trouble finding what he wanted on the Net because he was unsure how to use it. Those who zip through library reference systems often forget how long these took before they got the hang of them. The Net is no different. You speed up in all departments once you get used to it.

Actually there are computers on the Net that do nothing else but find things for you. Many of them use a file search program called Archie that runs around every so often making an index of what's available on the other computers.

This, of course, leaves you with the problem of finding those computers that run Archie.

The easiest way to do so is to get hold of a piece of software called Anarchie which has the Archie addresses built in. Another program called WS Archie does much the same thing.

Programs like these link you with Archie so you can hunt for the files you want and download them on to your hard disk. They're easy to use provided you know the full, accurate name of the file you want.

On the **World Wide Web** [P.48], one of the most useful search addresses is:

www.yahoo.com.

Yahoo lets you search by category, covering headings like Arts, News, Recreation and Sports, Entertainment, Music and so on.

Yahoo also offers links to other search engines like Open Text, Alta Vista, WebCrawler, Lycos, DejaNews, etc. They all do the same thing, but approach the job in different ways, so you can try them out to find which one you want.

TV's Discovery Channel backs an on-line personal researcher called Knapsack that keeps on working even after you log off.

You can find Knapsack by pointing your Web browser at

http://bbs.online.discovery.com/dcol/knapsack.

When you come to the Registration page, hit the button marked Register to create a new account, then make up any password you want.

Once you've registered you ask the program to search for files containing references to the subject that interests you – Oasis, for example, or the Man in the Moon. Then you log off and let it get on with the job.

Check your personal 'knapsack' in a day or two for a list of what the search has turned up and check out the files for yourself. Knapsack will even send you an **e-mail** P.43 every time it finds more of what you've been looking for.

Section Eight
THINGS THAT MIGHT FIND YOU ON THE NET

Things that might find you on the Net

Site 34 — The plague pit

▶ A computer virus is a small, vicious program written for an evil – or at least an antisocial – purpose. It is specially designed to infect the operating systems of computers and produce annoying or downright destructive effects.

The results of a virus infestation vary enormously. Sometimes it is nothing more serious than an unexpected random beep. Sometimes the only sign is increasingly sluggish performance. But other viruses are more sinister, working to corrupt your system or make your computer completely unusable.

Frequently a virus will lurk in your machine patiently waiting for a specific event or time. 1 April is a favourite. The program monitors the computer's internal clock and when the fateful day arrives it interrupts whatever you're doing to flash the message APRIL FOOL.

Unlike biological viruses, a computer virus can not be caught from the air. These little programs must be introduced into your system. There are only two ways this can be done.

> *'TROJAN HORSE – a virus-type program that masquerades as something else until you run it.'* – from a variety of virus descriptions posted on the Net.

One is by plugging in a floppy disk.

If you are in the habit of exchanging software with your friends via floppies, you run the risk of infection. Any virus present on the disk – usually attached to some piece of software on it – will jump to your machine.

Disk-based commercial software is usually clean, but not always. A London University student traced a virus infection on his Apple Mac to a chess program he bought from an established computer store. The program was clean when it went into stock in the store, but a salesman had tested the disk on the store's own computer to make sure it was working properly. The store system was infected, the virus jumped to the disk and hence to the student's Mac.

The second way to introduce a virus into your system is by downloading. It is probably true to say that 90 per cent or more of all computer virus infections are spread via the Internet.

Infection is without a doubt one of the greatest dangers of Net usage. There is almost no chance to trace the source of a particular Net virus and even when one is rooted out, there are scores more waiting to take its place. Some are vicious indeed. Downloaders of a set of glamour pictures some years ago found their hard disks erased when they tried to view them.

Since there seems no way of cleaning up the Net itself, virus protection software is strongly recommended before you go on-line, preferably the 'Watchdog' variety which checks downloads as they happen and blocks viral entry rather than cleaning up viral infection after it has actually taken hold.

Another Net problem Site 35 ▶
◀ Site 31 **Another Net problem**
Another Net problem Site 38 ▶

THINGS THAT MIGHT FIND YOU ON THE NET

Site 35 — Masters of Deception

▶ The Masters of Deception were a New York gang with names like Acid Phreak, Scorpion, The Wing and Phiber Optic.

It wasn't a street gang. These teenagers never saw a flick knife. Their weapons were computers. They used souped-up Commodore 64s with primitive **modems** P.29, and they taught themselves to be the most sophisticated hackers in the world.

They used to go trashing, which means crawling around in the rubbish, looking for computer print-outs that list secret passwords and log-on codes. These codes were keys to their chosen kingdom.

One of them, real name Paul, cut his teeth on software piracy. These were the days when software publishers still thought they could stop kids copying the games they bought. Paul loved the challenge. He loved figuring out what gimmicks the publishers were putting on the disks and most of all he loved finding ways around them. Hacking was in his blood.

After a while Paul got to hear about something called 'phone phreaking'. The story is there was a toy whistle given away with breakfast cereal. If you went into a public phone box and blew this whistle down the phone the right number of times, you were connected with the number you were calling for free. Kids all over America started making free calls. Some of them even learned how to get the right pitch without using the whistle.

Phone phreaking doesn't work any more. It was stopped by the installation of digital exchanges. But it gave Paul – and several other members of what would become the Masters of Deception – a deep and abiding interest in the telephone system.

The Internet

> *Hacker Kevin Poulsen was released on probation in 1996 after serving a five-year jail sentence for blocking the phone lines to radio stations so he could win competition prizes. He has now been told he must pay the equivalent of £40,000 in damages.*

In America and just about everywhere else now, the phone system is run by computers. It's linked into the Net, of course, since nearly all Net traffic travels along phone lines, but it's also a computer network in its own right.

Its various nodes (called switches) and customer files are heavily protected by special security codes. Back in the Eighties, when the gang began to operate, the management thought the system was fireproof. Some of their codes had *multi-million* combinations. If somebody wanted to crack them, he'd have to spend years dialling different combinations on the basis of trial and error.

What they didn't realize was that technology meant it wouldn't be a *person* dialling the numbers. Young people in electronic gangs like the Masters of Deception used to write programs that would have their computers try every combination of a security code.

Suppose you knew it was a ten digit code. The program would dial 0000000000. If that didn't get through, it would dial 0000000001. Then 0000000002. Then 0000000003. And so on, and so on.

Every so often, the program would find a code combination that allowed it to get through. It would then break the connection and make a note of the code. Paul and the boys used to leave these programs running all night, sometimes for days on end. It was like trawling for fish. You'd come down in the morning, check your computer and find you had a list of security codes you could use for hacking through the phone system.

> *'The punishments meted out to hackers are far too severe for the crime.'* – headline on a Sunday Times article by David Hewson in which he points out that sentences for hacking are sometimes more severe than those for manslaughter.

Of course, having made a connection, you were sometimes asked for a password. But since the management thought the system was fireproof, the passwords were often easy to remember, hence easy to guess. Paul used to try *test*, *guest* and even *password* and most of the time one of them got him through. Sometimes just hitting RETURN or ENTER on his computer keyboard did the trick.

Between trashing and code cracking and swapping codes and passwords with other hackers, the Masters of Deception were soon able to surf the phone system as easily as they could swagger down East 45th Street.

One of the first things they did was make sure the lines they were using never got charged for the calls they made. To do this, they broke into phone company files (called 'philes' in hacker jargon) and fiddled with the digits so what was actually an ordinary domestic line looked like one of the special lines the phone companies give to top executives who get to make free calls.

Eventually the lads managed to break into the philes that stored the technical manuals used by the engineers who had to repair breakdowns in the network. These manuals contained *all* the necessary codes. For hackers, it was like falling into Aladdin's Cave.

> *A Slovenian hacker released a virus on alt.sex, alt.crackers and alt comp. shareware newsgroups. It overwrote your hard drive while chanting 'HD Euthanasia by Demon Emperor: Hare Krishna, hare hare hare Rama...' About 200 PCs went down under the onslaught. The person responsible is thought NOT to be a member of the International Society for Krishna Consciousness.*

Once you're this deep into the phone system, you're into everywhere. The boys hacked into USENET, into TYMNET, into the Bank of America, into just about anywhere they wanted to go. They hacked into people's credit files. Once one of them called a station that was screening a discussion programme about hacking and told millions how much money the presenter had in his account.

> *'Money is just a type of information. As the information of money swishes around the planet, it leaves in its wake a history of its flow. If any of that complex flow can be anticipated, then the hacker who cracks this pattern will become a rich hacker, indeed.'* – Kevin Kelly.

Sometimes they got nasty. One hacker wrote a little program using UNIX commands designed to persecute people he didn't like. This program would instruct the computer to call your home number. When you answer the phone there's silence, so you hang up. The program calls you again. You answer again. Silence. Hang up. *Ring, ring*. Answer. Silence. Hang up. *Ring, ring*. On and on, hour after hour. Your phone never stops ringing. You answer it, there's nothing, you hang up and immediately it rings again.

The name of the program was *.annoy*.

Masters of Deception got busted fairly soon after 15 January, 1990, the day the entire AT&T telephone system collapsed right across America. It was a disaster which, rightly or wrongly, the Secret Service blamed on hacker activity.

So Acid Phreak and Phiber Optic aren't in business any more, but a few hundred thousand other hackers certainly are and the Internet is their happy hunting ground.

How hot could hacking get? Site 36 ▶

Site 36 — Cyberwar

▶ The Third World War will not be fought with atomic weapons or plastic tanks or even guns and soldiers. It will be fought on the Internet and, while not a drop of blood will be spilt, the consequences for the losing side will be disastrous.

Who says so? The Brussels Conference on Information Warfare in the European Community.

Delegates at the Conference concluded that Information Warfare was a global challenge facing all developed nations – and particularly the most advanced. It also represented 'the easiest and cheapest way for less developed nation states and religious and political movements to anonymously and grievously attack major nations and international corporations.'

The prediction sounds ominous, but what does it really mean? What is Information Warfare?

> *'In my opinion, infowar was dreamt up by story hungry journalists and PhDs with books to sell. In any case it's not hacking, merely vandalism. No reputable or skilled hacker would be involved with it.'* – 'Cold Fire' pseudonym for the individual described as the 'most notorious British hacker' as quoted by Ilsa Godlovitch in her investigation into UK hacking.

The term, which began to be used in high official circles a few years ago, is based on the recognition that the more sophisticated the economy of a country, the more it relies on electronic communications – the same communications that are now linked together in the Internet.

This reliance means that a country no longer has to attack an enemy's cities and factories with bombs. It can damage them just as effectively – and a lot more cheaply – by hacking into its communications networks and getting them from the inside.

Computer security expert Dr Neil Barrett predicts that 'infoterrorism' may be even more likely than all-out cyberwar – and could be as close as the year 2000.

'The absolute worst a hacker could do is plan a series of logic bombs for the millennium – hit the infrastructure simultaneously at several different points,' he said. 'All hell would break loose.'

Logic bombs are virus-like programs that force computers into a paradox loop, effectively shutting them down completely.

◀ Site 35 **How far hacking has already gone**

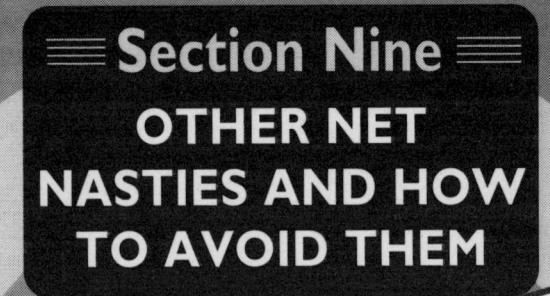

Section Nine
OTHER NET NASTIES AND HOW TO AVOID THEM

OTHER NET NASTIES AND HOW TO AVOID THEM

Site 37 — Romantic encounter

▶ Manchester schoolboy Aiden Thorley (not his real name) was 13 years old when he started using **Internet Relay Chat** P.68. He was 14 when he met the girlfriend of his dreams.

Aiden's father worked as an executive for one of the larger computer companies. A perk of his job was unlimited Internet access from both work and home workstations. But the last thing he wanted when he came back exhausted in the evenings was to sit down at yet another computer, so most of the surfing done in the Thorley household was by Aiden.

Aiden himself was intelligent but shy. He'd started to take an interest in girls, but by the end of his first year at high school, he was rapidly coming to the conclusion no girl was ever going to take an interest in *him*. The main problem (so he believed) lay in the fact that he was no good at sports. Any girls he knew seemed to be in love with the First XV rugby team.

As a result, Aiden became more introverted and withdrawn. After a while, he was so sure girls wouldn't like him that he became frightened of trying to make friends with them in the first place.

Aiden compensated by surfing the Net. He loved the **World Wide Web** P.48. Most evenings after supper he logged on and stayed following up hyperlinks until bedtime. Soon he was spending so much time on the Web that his mother started to worry. But his father was less concerned and since Aiden's school work didn't seem to suffer, neither of them tried seriously to curb his Internet interest.

One night Aiden actually overheard his father tell his mother that the Web 'might actually be good for the boy'

THE INTERNET

since it gave him access to up-to-date information for school projects and personal research. After that, Aiden took pains to foster the myth that he was really working when he was surfing.

About six weeks before his 14th birthday, Aiden accidentally stumbled on the Web page located at *www.xs4all.nl/~ircle/*. It was the home page for something called Ircle and at first glance it made no sense to him at all. But he accessed a FAQ (Frequently Asked Questions) page and discovered Ircle was chat software for the Macintosh.

> *The ultimate in computer dating is available on the Web. Just answer a series of questions about your ideal partner and you'll be matched up instantly ... with a character from The Simpsons.*

Aiden then followed links that took him to the home pages of the major **IRC** P.68 networks and suddenly discovered there was a whole world of live chat going on across the Internet. He downloaded the software he needed before going to bed and the next night took his first hesitant steps into this brave new venture.

He loved it almost from the start. The big thing was that nobody could see him so nobody would notice his pimples or his skinny build. And since nobody knew him, he could tell people only as much or as little about himself as he wanted them to know. He found to his surprise that even on channels normally used by people twice his age and more, his opinions were taken far more seriously than they were by adults face to face.

But Aiden was less interested in talking to adults than he was to people his own age. He began to move more and more into the specialized teen chat channels.

The first thing he discovered was teenagers on certain channels seemed to discuss little else but sex. This was a novelty for him at first, but after a while he got a bit tired of it and sometimes some of the conversations made him feel uneasy. All the same, it was nice to be talking freely to people his own age. After a while he noticed he was feeling a bit less self-conscious face to face as well. Not much, but a bit.

He was a real expert on IRC by the time he met Nightingale.

Aiden liked her almost from the start. She wasn't as heavily into sexy talk as some of them, but more importantly, she seemed far more interested in finding out about *him* than boasting about herself (which was a problem about a few others he'd met on the Net). It wasn't long before Aiden typed in /WHO IS NIGHTINGALE? to find out more about his new friend.

What he found out delighted him. Nightingale was the same age as him – two months older, actually, but he felt he could safely ignore that. Her real name was Karen and she had a UK e-mail address.

Over the next few weeks, Aiden chatted with Karen every night. Although she still seemed more interested in him than in talking about herself, he gradually wheedled out information on her likes and dislikes, her interests and her background. Soon he came to think he'd got to know her pretty well. One of the things he got to know was that she didn't have a steady boyfriend.

Two months after the start of their electronic relationship, Karen dropped the bombshell. Although Aiden had told her where he lived and where he went to school, Karen had flatly refused to reveal similar information about herself. Now, for the first time, she admitted she lived in Manchester too ... and suggested they should meet.

> Among the e-zines (electronic magazines) available on the Internet one is called Swoon. Heavily American in flavour, it covers 'dating, mating and relating'.

Aiden got so excited at the prospect that his appetite nose-dived. This attracted the attention of his mother, who must have told his father because Aiden found himself given a parental Third Degree that weekend.

He was reluctant to say too much about Karen, but they got it out of him eventually – including the fact that he and Karen planned to meet.

Aiden was surprised by how his parents took the news. His mother obviously thought the fact he'd found himself a girlfriend was 'sweet'. His father took a very different view.

At first, Mr Thorley flatly forbade him to go through with the meeting. Then, when that led to a stand-up row with the astonished Aiden, he insisted on going along.

The last thing Aiden wanted was to have his father along on his first date, but Mr Thorley was adamant.

Eventually they reached a painful compromise. Mr Thorley would come along, but remain in the background and would not expect to be introduced to Karen. Frankly, Aiden couldn't see why the old man was making so much fuss. It wasn't as if Aiden was a child any more – he'd now turned 14.

Aiden was nearly 20 minutes early for his date, which was to take place in a quiet little suburban coffee shop fairly close to his school. Aiden sat near the door beside a window. His father lurked in a corner, hidden – at Aiden's insistence – behind a morning newspaper.

OTHER NET NASTIES AND HOW TO AVOID THEM

Although Aiden would never have believed it until his date arrived, he was very glad to have his father's back-up. 'Karen' turned out to be a middle-aged man with a special interest in young boys.

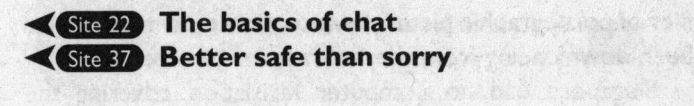

◀ Site 22 **The basics of chat**
◀ Site 37 **Better safe than sorry**

THE INTERNET

Site 38 — Sex crimes

▶In September 1996, police raided the home of a man in Singapore following a tip-off from Interpol and seized his computer equipment. His hard disk was found to contain files of pornographic pictures which, police claimed, he had been downloading from the Internet for two years.

Singapore had no computer legislation covering the situation, but the man was eventually charged under laws which banned obscene movies in the colony. Some of the material downloaded was animated and the Courts ruled this brought it within the existing law.

This is believed to be the first time anyone, anywhere, was prosecuted for downloading pornographic material for personal use, although a few months earlier a man in England was charged with possession of illegal pornography featuring young children which he had, as it happened, downloaded from the Net.

There are a large number of sites on the **World Wide Web** P.48 which carry files of pornographic pictures, text and movie clips for downloading. Some of these sites are commercial – you have to pay money via a credit card before you can access them – but many are not.

They contain material that goes far beyond the sort of pictures featured in men's magazines. What you find at these sites is hard core of the hardest type, including images of incest, extreme violence and child sexual abuse.

> *Every survey so far taken indicates that in terms of traffic, pornographic sites are the most popular places on the Net.*

Explicit sexual material is also a feature of several newsgroups.

OTHER NET NASTIES AND HOW TO AVOID THEM

The easy availability of pornography is perhaps the most frequent criticism levelled at the Internet and with good reason. There is a convention throughout the British Isles that newsagents place 'adult' magazines on their top display shelves to keep them out of reach of children. But no similar policy has been adopted by the Net.

There is nothing to stop a child of eight surfing intentionally or accidentally into a site containing the most extreme material – and it does happen. An incident in Ireland, which still maintains more rigid censorship regulations than the United Kingdom, illustrates the point.

A Dublin executive, who relies on his computer for his work, suffered from a head crash in his disk drive and borrowed another machine from a colleague to help him cope with the emergency. The colleague furnished him with a drive belonging to his young son, a boy of ten.

When the executive accessed the disk, he found folders stuffed with hard-core porn the boy had downloaded from various Net sites. His parents had been totally unaware of his activities.

In 1996, Superintendent Mike Hoskins, who heads the Metropolitan Police Clubs and Vice Unit, told representatives of UK service providers that if the industry did not take action to deal with the problem of Net pornography, the police would be forced to intervene.

The **service providers** P.33 later received a list of 143 **newsgroups** P.52 which the police wanted removed from their servers.

Police forces internationally are even more worried about the use of instant – and widespread – Internet communications in the organization of child sexual abuse rings. Pederasts are known to maintain information on the Net about the availability of victims, the location of clubs and the availability of child sexual services in the form of prostitution, brothels and illegal vice rings.

In America, the problem has been met with the principle of fighting fire with fire – police services are themselves now using the Net to co-ordinate their fight against child molesters and there are signs that British and European forces will soon follow suit.

> *Child pornography on the Net was top topic at the world's first conference on the sexual exploitation of children at Stockholm, Sweden in the summer of 1996.*

Pornography and paedophilia are not the only dangers to children represented by the Net. The adventurous child who downloads porn could also stumble on the formula for do-it-yourself explosive, diagrams on how to make a zip gun, mail order houses that sell flick-knives with no questions asked, instructions on experiments with acid and just about anything else you could name.

There is even a persistent rumour that plans for an A-bomb have been posted on the Net, but even if this is a myth there is certainly enough on-line to help you lose an eye, an arm or a life.

The easy access to unsavoury material has provoked substantial public debate for a number of years and recent times have seen some practical moves to combat the problem.

One of the first organizations to take steps was CompuServe, the largest of the commercial nets within the Net which announced that while it was not in the business of censoring its clients' activities, the service would not assist them in reaching questionable Internet sites. As a CompuServe customer, you could still freely surf the Net, but if you wanted porn, you had to search it out on your own.

This proved not to be enough. Towards the end of 1995, CompuServe temporarily suspended access to more than 200 **newsgroups** P.52 in response to a direct mandate from the prosecutor's office in Germany. Each of the newsgroups suspended was identified by the German authorities as illegal under German criminal law.

In a Press release, the company pointed out that while CompuServe had to comply with the laws of the many countries in which it operated, laws in different countries were often in conflict.

The statement added that CompuServe was investigating ways to restrict user access to selected newsgroups by geographical location.

Germany is only one of many countries that have introduced or plan to introduce laws against Internet pornography.

But there's a case against censorship   Site 39 ▶

THE INTERNET

Site 39 — Legislation and the Net

> 'What the Net is, more than anything else at this point, is a platform for entrepreneurial activities – a free-market economy in its truest sense. It's a level playing field where people can do anything they want to.'
> Marc Andreessen

▶ Moves to control the Internet in the United States were sparked by an NBC television feature in the summer of 1994 about on-line paedophiles. After considerable wrangling, the US government passed the Communication Decency Act in January, 1996.

The legislation did not have an easy ride. On Tuesday 12 December 1995, over 20,000 Net users flooded key members of Congress with phone calls, faxes and **e-mail** P.43 messages urging them to oppose it. Most of them believed that the personal freedom on which America was founded would be compromised if access were limited to certain types of material.

Despite the opposition, US law now states that anyone who 'makes, transmits, or otherwise makes available any comment, request, suggestion, proposal, image or other communication' which is 'obscene, lewd, lascivious, filthy or indecent' using a telecommunications device is liable to prosecution with penalties ranging up to $250,000 and up to two years' imprisonment.

Anyone anywhere who finds offensive material on the Internet can ask for the person who posted it to be prosecuted.

For 48 hours after President Clinton signed the bill, thousands of **World Wide Web** P.48 pages went black in a protest to show the impact of the new law. But Government bodies worldwide applauded the US stand and many moved to introduce similar laws.

> *'It's like illiterates telling you what to read.'* – writer Louis Rossetto commenting on moves by American politicians to censor the Internet.

The Australian Federal Government admits it has a responsibility to take action in the area of content control. The New South Wales state government released plans for Internet Censorship in April, 1996. The proposed legislation made it 'an offence to transmit, advertise [or] permit access to and retrieval of ... pornography and explicit material on the Internet'. Penalties of fines up to $10,000 for individuals and $25,000 for corporations will apply to offenders. Similar laws were already in place in the state of Victoria.

Not all laws of this type have been passed. In France in 1996, the *Conseil Constitutionnel* declared certain provisions of the Telco Act which sought to control the Internet were unconstitutional.

Worse still, not all – some would argue not any – laws of this nature are enforceable. In the late autumn of 1996, an international police operation led to the arrest of a man in the UK who had not only been sexually abusing children, but had actually used the Internet to distribute detailed descriptions of his actions to fellow paedophiles. The arrest was widely publicized, giving the impression of a clampdown, but (in private at least) very few law enforcement authorities really believe firm control of Internet pornography is remotely possible.

The problem is not just the volume of traffic on the Net, the sheer impossibility of monitoring individual phone communications into multi-millions of homes, or the political implications of any attempt to do so. The real complication is that governments can only make laws for their own countries, and the Internet is international.

◄ Site 38 **Why the laws are needed**
Why they aren't Site 41 ►

Site 40 — Safe surfing

▶While recognizing that unsuitable sites exist, most schools and public libraries offering Internet access to young people have not tried to limit access – something virtually impossible given the sheer size of the Net – but try to tackle the problem by requiring students to use the Internet responsibly.

This approach has become formalized in America where at least one Department of Education requires schools to accept guidelines for Internet use if they want to get grants. Students found violating the policy are simply banned from using the school's computers.

In more general guidelines issued by groups concerned with safe surfing for children, emphasis is placed on personal responsibility rather than legislation, censorship or other forms of Government intervention.

This approach points out that parents can teach children safe behaviour on the Internet just as they teach them to deal with the dangers of crossing the road or playing with fireworks.

> *'We believe the benefits of using the Internet far outweigh the risks of encountering offensive materials. We strongly encourage parents and schools to provide Internet access for their children!' – from Child Safety on the Internet at World Wide Web page http://omni.voicenet.com/~cranmer/censorship.html*

THE INTERNET

A page on Child Safety on the **World Wide Web** P.48 suggests the following point by point approach:

☐ Schools should develop acceptable user policies which establish clear guidelines for acceptable and unacceptable behaviour.

☐ All new users should be taught to use common courtesy whenever they participate in networking activities.

☐ All concerned networkers need to act responsibly and encourage their peers to do likewise.

☐ Inappropriate activities should be dealt with in a manner which respects the privacy, intellectual freedom and human rights of all concerned.

In a brochure entitled *Child Safety on the Information Highway*, Lawrence J. Magid gets a little more specific. He suggests that just as children learn the Rules of the Road, they should be taught the following six rules of an Information Superhighway Code:

1 I will not give out personal information such as my address, telephone number, parents' work address/telephone number, or the name and location of my school without my parents' permission.

2 I will tell my parents right away if I come across any information that makes me feel uncomfortable.

3 *I will never agree to get together with someone I 'meet' on-line without first checking with my parents. If my parents agree to the meeting, **I will be sure that it is in a public place and bring my mother or father along.***

4 *I will never send a person my picture or anything else without first checking with my parents.*

5 *I will not respond to any messages that are mean or in any way make me feel uncomfortable. It is not my fault if I get a message like that. If I do I will tell my parents right away so that they can contact the on-line service.*

6 *I will talk with my parents so that we can set up rules for going on-line. We will decide upon the time of day that I can be on-line, the length of time I can be on-line, and appropriate areas for me to visit. I will not access other areas or break these rules without their permission.*

If all else fails, both parents and institutions can fall back on the Internet control software that has become widely available. Packages like *Surfwatch* or *CyberSitter* allow children to log on to the Net but block access to sites that do not meet with parental approval.

This sort of software works one of two ways: by locking youngsters out of known sites their parents don't approve of; and by limiting access to those sites that their parents do. The two sound much the same, but aren't.

In the former case, the surfer has access to the entire Net with the exception of certain specified sites. Clearly this is not a foolproof way of protecting children from pornography since they may come across unsuitable sites of which their parents had no knowledge.

In the latter case, the surfer has access only to sites specified by the parents, which is foolproof in terms of protection, but only by denying the freedom of exploration that is among the greatest benefits of the Net.

OTHER NET NASTIES AND HOW TO AVOID THEM

Site 41 — **The case against censorship**

▶Despite the problems of **pornography** P.126, there is an international resistance to the imposition of censorship on the Net. Surfers have become accustomed to the old anything-goes attitude where self-responsibility and self-policing are everything. Many of them deeply resent any attempt to tell them what information they may or may not access.

In America, the Academic Council Committee on Libraries believes that access to Internet information should be subject only to financial limits and things like the useful life of the materials, storage capacity and so on. No other limits should be imposed.

> With an estimated readership of 350,000, the newsgroup alt.sex is more popular than any other except news.announce.newusers.

The argument is that while views may be expressed that seem wrong, distasteful or offensive, this is the nature of the freedom to consider new ideas.

In a free and open student situation, no idea should be banned or forbidden and no viewpoint held to be so hateful or disturbing that it might not be expressed.

According to this viewpoint, rules that ban or punish speech based upon its content cannot be justified. We should always distinguish between what we dislike and what we outlaw.

In an on-line talk on 'Sex, Censorship and the Net', educator Carl Kadie outlined the following scenario to illustrate the problems of censorship:

You are a professor at an American university who has established a free public access computer service linked to the university.

After it has been running for a while, the local paper reports that your service is carrying a paedophile **newsgroup** P.52 that frequently posts illegal material.

The question you have to consider is whether or not you kill the newsgroup.

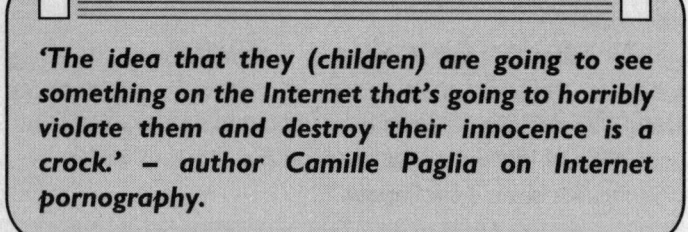

> *'The idea that they (children) are going to see something on the Internet that's going to horribly violate them and destroy their innocence is a crock.'* – author Camille Paglia on Internet pornography.

According to Kadie, the Library 'Bill of Rights' says that 'materials should not be proscribed or removed because of partisan or doctrinal disapproval'. This means you shouldn't remove or ban postings just because they're offensive – even if they're offensive to you. By that criterion, the offending newsgroup should stay.

There is, of course, another view. This view holds that young people especially are in need of protection. A paedophile newsgroup is likely to attract active child molesters and may become a cover for the setting up of a paedophile ring. Even if this is not the case, the posting of illegal material must, by law, be prevented.

The sting in the tail of Kadie's talk was that such a newsgroup actually existed and had not been taken off-line by its system operator.

The subject under discussion has been whether paedophilia could ever be acceptable in society or whether it was downright evil.

Opponents of Net censorship are generally opposed to legislation in the area. They claim these laws don't just infringe free speech in general, but specifically limit the freedom of those they seek to protect.

They also point to the problem of what should be censored. Are governments – including repressive totalitarian governments – really entitled to decide what information their citizens should have?

Declaration of Independence in Cyberspace.

1 The Internet is a unique communications medium which deserves protections at least as broad as those afforded to print, television and radio media.

2 Individual users and parents, not the Government, should determine for themselves and their children what material comes into their homes based on their own tastes and values.

3 That these [proposed new] laws [in America, Australia and elsewhere] will be ineffective at protecting children from 'indecent' or 'patently' offensive material on-line.

– Taiss Quartapa.

In the (comparatively) more liberal West, there is a feeling that initial Internet legislation against pornography is almost bound to be the thin end of a very dangerous wedge, opening the door for further laws restricting the way we talk, work, think, show or otherwise interact on any on-line medium.

Australian Taiss Quartapa says in an on-line article on the subject, 'It's not that I approve of such things ... as child pornography or material that describes recipes for creating napalm. I do, however, believe that if these people want to share this material with each other, they should be allowed to do so without fear of persecution. Persecute the perpetrators – not those who view the material.'

The belief among the anti-censorship lobby is that the Internet can regulate itself, creating its own standards, changing its technology and developing 'lock-out' software that allows parents to control what their children see.

They point out that the Internet is bigger than a single state or country ... and possibly more powerful. Perhaps it is for this reason that governments are adding new laws – for their own protection, rather than the community's.

◀ Site 39 **The legislative approach**
◀ Site 40 **Safety codes for the Net**

Section Ten
DANGEROUS ADVENTURES

Site 42 — A brief history of MUD

▶In fantasy role-play games, players act out a scenario run by a sort of referee known as a games master. The scenario itself is often derived from fantasy stories the players know about — monsters from *Lord of the Rings* and that sort of thing.

The players act out roles as warriors, wizards, clerics, thieves and so forth. The game is a drama that depends on the creative imagination of the players along with dice rolls that say whether you've won the fight or crossed the chasm or stolen the magic orb or whatever it was you were trying to do.

The original fantasy role-play game is the still-popular *Dungeons and Dragons*.

In the days when 'computer' meant mainframe, somebody wrote a program called *Colossal Cave* which was to waste more time for students and scientists than virtually any other piece of software at the time.

Colossal Cave was the first computer adventure game. It was text only, no graphics at all, so like *Dungeons and Dragons* you more or less played it in your head. It said things like *You are standing at a crossroads*. You then keyed in N (for north), S (for south) and so on to tell the program where you wanted to go. It then told you what happened when you did.

After a while you found yourself in a colossal cave, picking up treasures and fighting orcs.

The *Colossal Cave* type of adventure came to the early PCs in the guise of games like *Zork*, which was billed with the wonderful advertising slogan *Your greatest adventure lies ahead ... and downwards*. *Zork* was text only when it hit the market (although they've brought out a graphic version now on CD).

The original *Zork* and *Colossal Cave* had a lot in common with *Dungeons and Dragons*. They were essentially head games. Their real power lay in the way they encouraged you to visualize. They weren't role-play, but in some respects they came a lot closer than later things like *Doom*.

As the Internet grew, some of its servers carried adventure games like *Colossal Cave*. They were far more suited to playing via a modem than graphic games because even now – and certainly then – graphics slow things down too much.

So, in the early days of the Net, you had hundreds of players wandering through their own individual adventures. From there it was a very short step to the idea of having those hundreds of players stay on-line and wander through the *same* adventure.

That way, they could interact with one another.

On-line adventure games were developed which married the old-style text adventures to the whole concept of role-play. When you logged on, you got to be a warrior or a wizard or a cleric or a thief, just like in *D&D*.

Many of the characters you met were generated by the computer, but some weren't. Some were human players just like you. You could team up with them, fight them, pit your wits against them, whatever.

The bottom line was you were all together in the most incredible fantasy adventure of your life.

These new Internet-based games were called Multi User Dungeons in deference to good old *D&D*. They're often referred to as MUDs for short.

Where to find some MUD   Site 43 ▶
When MUD turns to quicksand   Site 44 ▶

Site 43 — Playing in the MUD

➤ The first thing you do when starting to explore a Multi User Dungeon is to pick your character. When you play one of these games, you're no longer yourself. Instead you get to be a warrior with a licence to kill, or a wizard who can cast spells, or a thief capable of moving so silently nobody can hear, or hiding in shadows so she's close to invisible.

In virtually all the many MUD versions, characters start off weak and inexperienced, but get a whole lot stronger if they manage to survive. Fighters become better able to kill – and find better weapons to do so. Wizards get more powerful magic. Everybody collects treasure. And so on.

Once you have your character, you're ready to enter the scenario. Typically it will have a medieval fantasy setting, so your weapons are more likely to be swords and spears than machine guns or laser rifles. Although the real goal is to enjoy, survive and prosper, you will very quickly be drawn into a specific adventure.

> *You can find a list of MUD sites by pointing your browser at:*
> *http://www.interplay.com/mudlist/.*
> *The Yahoo search site at the near impossible address:*
> *www.yahoo.com/text/Recreation/Games/Internet_Games/MUDs_MUSHes_MOOs_etc_/*
> *will also set you going.*

This might be a quest to find some great and powerful object, like a magical crystal or the Holy Grail. It might be an attempt to rid a village of a dragon feeding on its maidens or a plague of demons called up by some evil sorcerer. It might be a treasure hunt triggered by the discovery of an ancient map. It might be the discovery of a gateway into another universe.

Whatever the plotline, the story never ends. As soon as you successfully meet one challenge, another arises to take its place. As your character grows in abilities, so you have the opportunity to get involved in more dangerous missions with bigger and better rewards.

In a MUD, you do not necessarily enter a scenario alone. You can do, but equally you can go in as part of a group pledged to help and support each another in this land of make-believe.

Alternatively, you can be one of a group of enemies determined to slaughter one another on sight.

Either way, you are going to make more friends and more enemies as you go along because there are scores of other players in there with you.

◀ Site 42 **How MUDs came to be**
Dangers in the MUD Site 44 ▶

DANGEROUS ADVENTURES

Site 44 — Sticking in the MUD

▶ The whole entertainment industry is built on the idea that people need to escape from their worries now and then. And while pop concerts and rave parties come in for criticism, you don't hear complaints about the ballet or the opera, which are just up-market ways of meeting the same need.

But maybe you can get too much of a good thing. There's an ongoing argument about television that centres not so much on *what* you should watch as *how much* you should watch. It's quite difficult to overdo the cinema where a limited number of movies are available even in large cities and costs have become quite high. But the television set is there all the time, pumping out pictures from early morning to late at night. Some stations are on air 24 hours a day.

The Internet is like that. The Internet never sleeps. You can log on just as easily at 4 a.m. as 6 p.m. You can surf the **Web** P.48 or join in the activities of a **Multi User Dungeon** P.143 as long as you can stay awake.

> *Recent research shows Net users watch less TV and read more newspapers and magazines than their non-surfing counterparts.*

There are some people who argue that the problem with MUDs – indeed with role-play in general – goes way beyond their individual fascination.

In the Bible Belt of America, for instance, there's a theory that when you imagine you're fighting demons in a dungeon, you're somehow opening a mystic gateway that could allow real demons to get into your head.

You may not have much time for this sort of thinking,

THE INTERNET

but it's less easy to laugh off the idea that role-play encourages the development of things in your personality that would have been better left alone.

This goes a bit beyond the idea that violence in the movies and on television encourages violence in the streets. With the movies and television, you're only watching Rambo. In a MUD (or any other sort of dungeon come to that) *you're* making the decision about when to slit somebody's throat.

But what makes a MUD particularly tricky is that there are other people in there with you — real living, breathing people just like you, controlling characters just like yours. It's not a huge step from having your character fight with their character to feeling it's the person behind the character who's your enemy.

In other words, the set-up of a MUD makes it that much easier to confuse fantasy with reality.

◀ Site 42 **How MUDs came to be**
Somebody who did confuse fantasy with reality Site 46 ▶

DANGEROUS ADVENTURES

Site 45 — Heroine addiction

▶ Is there anything much wrong with escaping from reality for a little while? The story of Sandy sounds a warning note.

Thirteen-year-old Sandy got her first boxed set of *Dungeons and Dragons* as a Christmas gift in 1983. She was delighted to have it. She'd heard about the game, which was making a lot of headway at that time, and wanted to find out what all the fuss was about.

On Boxing Day, four friends and Sandy started to set up their characters. The procedure was complicated and took most of the afternoon. She found it frankly tedious. Certainly there was nothing in what they were doing to explain why the game had become so popular.

They started their first scenario around 5 o'clock. Sandy figured if the game was as good as it was cracked up to be, it might take them through the evening.

Sometime in March, 1984, she stopped to take stock of her position. She had played *Dungeons and Dragons* every day, seven days a week, for over two months! Her homework had suffered. Her school work had suffered. Even her leisure time activities – she enjoyed dancing and had started ballet training – had suffered.

Even then, she didn't stop playing *Dungeons and Dragons*. She just slowed down. Eventually she got it under control and role-play became more of a sideline than a career.

> *Only about one third of Net users are currently female, but this is changing rapidly.*

Until, that is, somebody gave her the computer game *Wizardry* for her birthday a year later.

The impact wasn't quite so bad this time, largely because she'd learned from experience. But it was bad enough. In *Wizardry* you create a full adventure party made up of several characters with differing talents.

Strictly speaking, since *Wizardry* is a personal computer game, you're expected to control all these characters yourself. But Sandy figured it might be even more fun to put together a group of players, each of whom would be responsible for controlling one character. She had interested friends and even her parents joined in as they had with *Dungeons and Dragons*.

That's not to say everybody took turns at the computer keyboard. What happened was each player told the keyboard operator what their character was going to do in any given set of circumstances. The keyboard operator would then punch in the relevant commands.

It was all about as close to a **Multi User Dungeon** P.143 as it was possible to get given the technology of the day. Sandy played regularly for months.

> *Researchers disagree radically about how much time the average user spends on the Net. Estimates vary from 2.5 to 6.6 hours a week.*

Once again her work schedule suffered and the others had their problems too. It wasn't just the time they actually spent playing *Wizardry* — they'd waste hours discussing what happened during their last session and planning cunning strategies for their next.

It was ridiculous, but it happened and it kept on happening until they reached the bottom level and overcame the wicked wizard.

What made *D&D* and *Wizardry* so massively appealing?

For Sandy, they both offered an escape into a fantasy world that was a lot more interesting, rewarding and exciting than the one she was living in the rest of the time. Life as a student had nothing on a world where magic worked, you got to kill people you disliked, there was gold for the taking and death could be cured by bribing a cleric to say the right sort of prayer.

In the alternative reality of role-play, Sandy was the heroine of a great, ongoing adventure. In short, it became a real addiction.

In the form of **MUDs** P.143 role-play is one of the most popular game types available on the Internet. It brings the risk of fantasy addiction to a wider audience than at any time in human history.

How big the risk of fantasy addiction can get Site 46 ▶
Internet addiction Site 47 ▶

THE INTERNET

Site 46 — Sinking in the MUD

▶ On 22 August 1979, an American private eye with the unlikely name of William Dear received a phone call from a prominent Texas surgeon called Melvin Gross. Gross's young nephew had disappeared and he wanted Dear to investigate. Dear asked a few questions, got interested and agreed to take the case.

The nephew who had disappeared was James Dallas Egbert III, a sixteen-year-old who had been taking a summer course at Michigan State University. Detective Dear soon discovered that Dallas, as he was known to his friends, had a measured IQ of 180 (the average is 100), well above genius level. He was a brilliant mathematician who impressed his professors and had no problems with his school work — one of the main reasons why teenagers sometimes run off.

When Dear arrived in East Lansing, where the Michigan State University is located, he found the Press were wondering about kidnapping. But as he began his investigation proper, he discovered people were talking about far more weird possibilities. There were rumours of witch cults and drug rings. Some even tried to link the boy's membership of the school's Gay Council to his disappearance.

> *'Other times I thought it would be better to disappear and not kill myself, disappear and never be seen again. I was being cruel at times like this ... It was just revenge against my mom and dad.'* – Dallas Egbert as quoted in William Dear's book, The Dungeon Master.

Dear visited the boy's room in Case Hall dormitory and read a note which had been left on top of some poems written by Dallas. The note, which was unsigned, read: 'To whom it may concern. Should my body be found, I wish it to be cremated.'

It looked like suicide, but William Dear didn't believe it. In his experience, teenagers who killed themselves wrote lengthy letters of explanation and left their rooms in a mess. Dallas's cremation note was far too short and his room was so tidy it was spooky.

Mr Dear wasn't happy with the kidnapping theory either. It would have been very difficult to abduct Dallas without being seen and, besides, laser and ultraviolet examination of the scene showed not even microscopic signs of a struggle.

When you're investigating a disappearance, it's always a good idea to find out as much as you can about the person who's disappeared – and not simply what sort of things he did, but also how he thought.

Dear discovered Dallas took drugs, some of which he actually manufactured himself. He also found the boy was a nut about **fantasy role-play** P.143. It was about all he ever talked about. A fellow student named Karen Byerly said Dallas once told her he wondered what it would be like to have a role-play type adventure in real life. Specifically he talked about a sophisticated game of hide and seek with real-life police trying to find him by following clues he had deliberately left.

What people say and what people do are very different things so Dear didn't necessarily accept this was what Dallas was up to now. But later he found some hard evidence that Dallas was capable of bringing role-play into the real world. It appeared he wasn't content with the head game – he liked to act out **FRP** P.143 scenarios in the maze of tunnels which carried steam pipes for the heating system beneath the school.

Dear wrote a book about the case called *The Dungeon Master*, published by Sphere in the UK, which gives the full story of the case. The bottom line was this:

Some time after he began his investigations, Dear got a middle-of-the-night phone call from the boy he was looking for.

Dallas at first refused to say where he was, but eventually admitted he was in Morgan City, Louisiana, nearly five hundred miles away. Dear flew out and collected him. The boy was physically okay, but seemed mentally shattered. He had been missing for nearly a month.

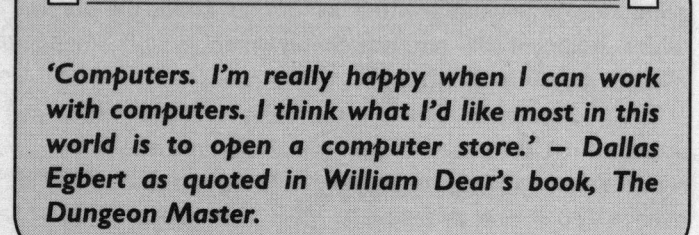

> *'Computers. I'm really happy when I can work with computers. I think what I'd like most in this world is to open a computer store.'* – Dallas Egbert as quoted in William Dear's book, *The Dungeon Master*.

Dallas told William Dear he'd been planning to disappear for almost a year. Sometimes he wanted to go off somewhere and kill himself – he didn't think anybody cared about him.

At other times he thought it would be better just to disappear and stay alive, sending a mysterious postcard every five years or so to the people he'd left behind.

One day he turned thought into action. He slipped into the tunnels underneath the school.

Dallas was very familiar with those tunnels. He'd been in them acting out role-play scenarios maybe 200 times and knew them like the back of his hand.

He told Dear, 'Playing the game – for real, I mean – was total escape. I mean, I could get into it. Scramble through those tunnels like a monkey... There's nothing to constrain you except the limit of your imagination.'

That night in the tunnels, Dallas made his bid to escape in the real world by taking an overdose of pills. It didn't work. He came to next morning, left the tunnels and stumbled to a friend's home about a mile away.

He stayed there for about a week before being passed on to another house, then another.

He was taking drugs most of the time and the people in the houses weren't exactly Methodist Ministers. Somebody in the third house gave him a bus ticket to Chicago and told him to take the train from there to New Orleans.

In New Orleans, Dallas made another attempt at suicide, drinking down some home-made cyanide mixed with root beer. It didn't work either, though it did make him sick as a dog.

He lived rough for a while, then met a man who told him he might be able to get work in Morgan City. While there he made a phone call to a friend in East Lansing, heard Dear was investigating his disappearance and decided to phone him.

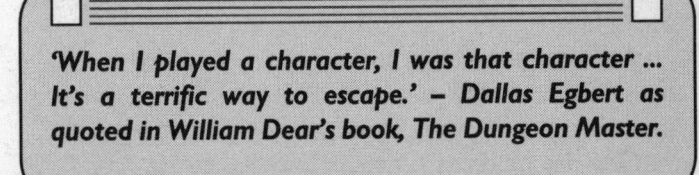

> 'When I played a character, I was that character ... It's a terrific way to escape.' – Dallas Egbert as quoted in William Dear's book, The Dungeon Master.

Dallas did not live happily ever after. On 11 August 1980, just under a year after his original disappearance, he shot himself through the head with an automatic pistol and died six days later.

A Publisher's Note at the beginning of William Dear's book makes the point that crawling about real tunnels is definitely not the way you'd normally play a fantasy role-play game. Nor is it recommended by the publishers of these games that you carry them over into real life. Sound advice.

It's also true that Dallas took drugs and associated with people who might reasonably be described as 'undesirable'. He seems to have been one of those kids with a lot of intelligence, but very little sense.

With such a complex personality, so many serious emotional problems and a distinct attraction towards suicide, it would be ridiculous to blame role-play for his death. But his obsession with role-play was so great that perhaps it contributed to it.

And role-play is now available to a wider audience than ever before thanks to **MUD** P.143 on the Net.

◀ Site 42 **How MUDs came to be.**

Site 47 — Internet addiction

▶ In June 1996, the *Sunday Times* reported the existence of a brand-new illness that had begun to ruin hundreds of lives. It was called **IAS**, short for **I**nternet **A**ddiction **S**yndrome.

Internet addiction is a very real condition, shown by an urgent need to log on the moment you wake up and recurring dreams and fantasies about the Net. Typically sufferers will lie to parents and friends about the amount of time they spend wired and will find it impossible to cut down when they realize something is wrong.

It sounds like a joke and the Webaholics Home Page (at: *http://cns-web.cns.ohiou.edu/~rbarrett/webaholics/ver2/* but looking for a new home at time of writing) treats it as such with links to interesting sites throughout the Net and the instruction:

Remember: Admitting that you have an addiction is the first step to finding more and more really cool web pages!

There is, however, an indication that a real problem may exist in the addendum: 'Note: If you really believe you are spending too much time on the **Web** P.48, perhaps it is time for some real help.'

Psychologists and psychiatrists certainly believe so. They quote horror stories of genuine addiction like that of the teenager who regularly logged on 12 hours a day and needed psychiatric help to break him of his habit.

Sometimes the condition can lead to tragedy, as in the case of a merchant seaman who ran up an almost unbelievable debt of £14,000 due to his addiction and eventually committed suicide.

THE INTERNET

> 'This is a bona fide disorder. These are not sad people who had unsatisfying lives. They are people whose lives were just fine before they found the Internet.' – Mark Griffiths, addictions expert at Nottingham Trent University.

Research has shown IAS follows the same pattern as better known addictions like smoking, gambling and alcohol. Those who suffer feel irritable, tense, depressed or restless if deprived of their Internet fix. Often there is neglect of responsibilities and an affect on physical or mental health.

Interestingly, the addiction is most likely to grip someone who has never used a computer before. Contrary to popular belief, the real computer addicts are not the young, but the middle-aged or elderly coming to the Internet for the first time.

IAS seems to have hit hardest in the United States where nearly a fifth of those who replied to a New York survey admitted spending a massive forty hours each week connected to the Net.

A psychiatrist with experience of the addiction warned against going cold turkey and advised that the time spent surfing should be limited to a set number of hours each day.

◀ Site 45 **Another Internet addiction**

Section Eleven

COMING SOON

Site 48 — The future of the Net

▶ Back in the 1940s a scientist announced that it was, and always would be, impossible to make a computer as small and complex as the human brain.

The only computer in existence then was ENIAC, which lit up 18,000 valves. The scientists pointed out that to house enough valves to match the human brain, you'd need a room ten times bigger than the Empire State Building and a water supply larger than Niagara Falls to keep them cool.

He was right too. His mistake was in thinking the future would be much like the present only more so.

If there's one thing you can be sure of, it's that the future isn't going to be anything like the present.

And that includes the future of the Internet.

You might be tempted to imagine by the time you're middle-aged you'll be sitting at your keyboard sending messages across a Net that reaches every human being on the globe.

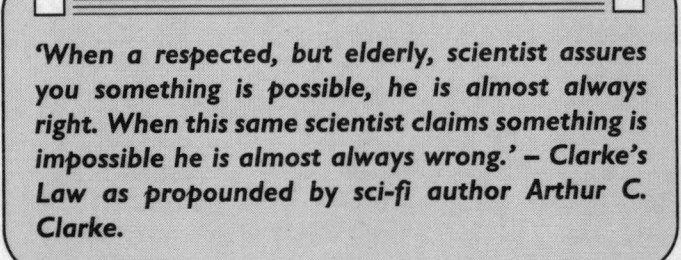

> *'When a respected, but elderly, scientist assures you something is possible, he is almost always right. When this same scientist claims something is impossible he is almost always wrong.'* – Clarke's Law as propounded by sci-fi author Arthur C. Clarke.

You might imagine **e-mail** P.43 will have replaced regular post.

You might imagine your computer will be neater, faster, far more powerful.

You might see your modem working around two billion bits per second, blasting data down a dedicated fibre-optic cable at light speed.

You might imagine downloading whole interactive movies where you control the captain of the *Starship Enterprise* and decide exactly what to do about those Klingons off the starboard bow.

But that's assuming the future will be much like the present only more so. The reality, almost certainly, will be very different.

It may even be virtual.

For the link to three alternative Net futures Site 52 ▶

COMING SOON

Site 49 — Virtual reality

▶ To get an idea what virtual reality's all about, cast your mind back to the last time you played a game like *Doom*, *Marathon*, *Pathways Into Darkness*, *Might and Magic*, *Ultima* or any of the **FRP** P.143 epics.

When you're in one of those games, you're operating in a fictional environment. But it works (more or less) the same way as a real one. It has roads and rivers, buildings, trees and mountains. If you want to follow the road to the right, you turn right. If you want to get into a building, you have to find a door. It isn't reality, but it might as well be. It's nearly real — it's *virtually* real.

That's why they've started talking about virtual reality. It's very nearly like the real thing and getting closer to it all the time.

The first virtual reality machines were the flight simulators used for training airline pilots. Climbing into one of these things is like climbing into the cockpit of a real aeroplane. All the controls, dials, warning lights and instruments are there and when you start the plane, you can hear the engine noise. Through the window you can see the runway and when you take off, your view (and your seat!) moves to give you the heady impression you're actually flying.

In a flight simulator, you can do anything you could do at the controls of a real plane – including crashing into the sea. It allows pilots to learn from their mistakes in an environment that puts nobody in any danger.

Flight simulators have been with us a long time. Virtual reality helmets and associated gear are much more recent.

Although it's not all that obvious, a virtual reality helmet is just as much a computer interface as a keyboard or a mouse. When you put it on, sensors pick up head movement so the helmet knows what you're looking at. A good one can fine-tune on eye movement as well. There's a joystick attached so you can signal when you want to walk forward or back or to the side. Advanced models put you on a sort of walkway.

That's what's *actually* happening. What seems to be happening is something else. When you put on the helmet, the first thing it does is cut you off from the rest of the world. You can no longer see or hear what's going on in the room you're in. Instead, you see and hear in a brand-new environment generated by the computer.

With cheap headsets, it's simplistic. It feels like you're playing a fairly crude computer game, except it's in 3-D and you're right in it. But you don't have to point and click. You turn your head to the right to see what's happening to your right. Turn your head to the left and you see what's happening over there. In fact, you can turn round the whole 360°. It's as if you fell into a whole new computer world. You'll hear in stereo and interact with computer-generated characters that look like real people.

When you forget about what's commercially on sale and get into the labs where they're developing this technology, you start to see how far it's likely to go. For example, in one US virtual reality lab you're given gloves as well as a headset.

These gloves have pressure pads wired into the computer so when you step into your virtual reality world and a computer generated character walks up to you and shakes hands, you can feel the handshake. The computer uses the pressure pads inside your gloves so your hand seems to feel his hand.

Most experts predict some form of virtual reality, combined with voice recognition, is likely to become the computer interface of the future. That means it will be the

Internet interface of the future as well. But even now, the Net is nudging towards virtual reality in **chat** P.68 environments like The Palace, virtual shopping malls and so on.

This trend is set to increase. In autumn 1996 Apple introduced a new software called HotSauce based on Meta Content Format indexing. HotSauce runs on both Macs and IBM PCs, which gives it almost universal application.

Using HotSauce, you describe what you want in a simple text file and the software translates it into a three-dimensional graphic environment. This leaves the way open to a revolution in the presentation of **World Wide Web** P.48 pages. Instead of using hypertext links within a site, the site itself is presented as a three-dimensional world you can move through, unearthing different information at different locations and levels, but never losing sight of the overall structure.

Software like HotSauce adds technical zip to the Internet's 3-D virtual reality standard which, again in autumn 1996, laid down some rules for the use of avatars.

An avatar, popularized in some Net chat services, is a sort of second personality you can use when visiting the Net. The standards introduced in 1996 mean you can surf the Net as a graphic representation which can go shopping, play games or engage in various different activities. The avatar is coded with details of who you really are, what you want to be called on the Net, the persona you've built up in various games, notably **MUDs** P.143 and, for wealthier surfers, things like credit card numbers.

> *All these developments are aspects of Cyberia, a whole new world currently being created in hyperspace by the interaction of Net computers and the introduction of increasingly sophisticated hardware and software.*

In line with these various developments, it has become possible to use bits of *virtual* reality in place of *real* reality.

A case in point is virtual money. All you need is an agreement between the parties that virtual money can be transformed, at some stage, into actual money.

There are already companies operating on the Net that have agreed to accept virtual cash. If you want to buy something from them, you use virtual money from your virtual account with, say, the First Virtual Bank of America.

The money is deducted from your virtual account and banked in the virtual account of the company you're buying from. It's just like an ordinary bank transaction. Since there are no credit card numbers flying around, there's nothing for a hacker to hack into – and it's virtually impossible to steal virtual cash.

The (fictional) transaction you had with the company gets real at the end of the month when the First Virtual Bank of America charges the cost of the transaction to your credit card account. You give them your credit card details by phone when you open your virtual account in the first place.

This is far safer than using a credit card on the Net where the quoted number could potentially pass through a thousand computers before reaching its destination. And at any of these stations a watchdog program could lurk waiting to catch the sequence of numbers typical of a credit card transaction.

How far VR could go Site 50 ▶

Site 50 — Ultimate interface

▶There's been a very interesting trend in the way we interact with computers. The early computers were a nightmare. You had to learn all sorts of obscure commands just to get them up and running. You had to learn more commands every time you bought a new piece of software. If you made one mistake, like a missing full stop or an invisible control character, your machine closed down and sulked.

After a while, there was a move towards something called a **GUI**, short for **G**raphic **U**ser **I**nterface. This was based on the idea that even if you couldn't spell Tyrannosaurus Rex, you'd recognize one if it bit you – or, more to the point, you'd recognize a picture of one if it came up on your screen.

Instead of the old DOS commands, the GUI used icons to show what your computer would do for you. You might have an icon of a printer to show it would print out text. Or an icon of a disk to show it would save material to disk. Or an icon of a rubbish bin to show you what to do with stuff you no longer wanted.

Along with the icons came a gizmo called a mouse which controlled a little arrow on your screen called a cursor. The sales people started to talk about the *intuitive* use of computers, because with icons and a mouse, you could often figure out how to work one without reading the manual.

COMING SOON

> *'Currently they're working on environments for news and reference, banking and finance, clubs and interests, travel and exploration, sports and adventure, education and learning and shopping etc.'* – Gareth Lancaster in an Internet article on virtual reality.

To help the intuitive user, they brought in metaphors to back up the icons. They decided to make the surface of your screen a metaphor for a desktop. They decided to make certain icons look like cardboard files so your computer turned into a metaphor for an office.

The whole idea was to make the way you used computers closer to the way you did everything else. The next step was obvious. Why not make using a computer *exactly* like the way you do everything else? Instead of having a *metaphor* for an office, make it that you walk into an *actual* office. Instead of having a little icon *metaphor* for a file, make it that you pick up an *actual* file.

In other words, go for **virtual reality** P.163.

There are already an increasing number of virtual reality sites on the Net itself and these will certainly grow. But what's at issue here is not the sites, but the overall interface. A virtual reality interface will transform the Net as a whole.

How far away is such an interface? There are scientists in the States and Japan working on something called 'smart skin'.

Smart skin is a sort of rubberized body stocking. You slip into this thing with gel and electrodes before you put on your VR goggles and phones.

Smart skin does two things. First, it registers *all* your body movements. So now instead of using a joystick to tell the computer you want to walk forward, you just ... walk forward.

The smart skin senses your movement, feeds that through to the computer and the computer changes the viewpoint in your VR world accordingly. The same thing happens if you reach out with one arm. The smart skin tells the computer what you're doing and the computer draws the virtual arm reaching out from your virtual body.

The second thing smart skin does is even more interesting. It feeds back to you any skin sensations the computer wants you to feel. And this is where virtual reality starts to leave the planet.

Picture a very simple scene. You're in a virtual reality room with a table and a chair. On the table is a bottle of Cola, a tray of ice cubes and an empty glass. You walk towards the table. Your perspective on the room changes as you move. You can hear the sound of your footsteps on the (virtually) wooden floor. You pull out the chair. The smart skin you're wearing makes you feel it. You sit down on the chair. You bend your knees and squat, but parts of the smart skin grow rigid so you're held in position. It feels exactly like you're sitting on the chair.

You reach for the tray of ice cubes. The smart skin draws heat from your fingers so you have the sensation that the ice cubes are cold. You drop a couple in the glass. You can hear them tinkle through your earphones. You pick up the bottle of Cola. The smart skin feeds you back the feel of the bottle, its exact weight and temperature. You pour the Cola...

At the moment, even smart skin won't let you *taste* the Cola. But they're working on that, the same way they're working on the problem of virtual odours.

The miracles of smart skin will eventually be replaced by an even more sophisticated interface.

The VPL Corporation is one of the more adventurous virtual reality interface design firms in California's Silicon Valley. It is currently working on a nerve chip that will allow your computer to communicate directly with your brain. This is part of a whole new approach to computer use called 'wireheading'.

Wireheading has a host of possibilities. It will probably start with you literally plugging wires into your head. But as the system becomes more sophisticated, you'll have a microchip and a tiny transmitter surgically implanted in your skull. Biological engineering will coax your brain cells to link themselves with silicon chips. Eventually, nanoengineering will allow organic matter to be incorporated into the chips themselves, so you can attach them directly to your nerve endings.

At this stage, even smart skin becomes obsolete. The computer will control your perception of reality by direct manipulation of your brain. This has *already* been done to some extent. In 1935, a neurosurgeon named Wilder Penfield inserted electrodes in a patient's brain and discovered he could cause her to relive moments out of her past.

During these episodes, she could see, hear, touch, taste and smell exactly as if what she was experiencing was physically real. Before long, Net surfers will be doing the same thing.

◀ Site 49 **Virtual reality basics**

THE INTERNET

> Site 51 — Passport to Cyberia

▶ They've already started talking about 'surfing cyberspace'. Cyberspace is that great abstract world of computer information accessible through the keyboard interface you use at present when you're wired into the Net.

Add virtual reality and suddenly cyberspace stops being an abstraction. It becomes Cyberia, a place. It's a place where you can see, hear and touch, just like any other. The only passport you need is the set of goggles, phones and smart skin.

This new world, Cyberia, functions like an alternate reality. Already on the Internet there are shopping malls and libraries, museums and software stores. In the Cyberian Internet, you will be able to fly directly to them – without a plane – then walk through virtual doors to examine the files and software packages for yourself.

When you visit the art galleries, it won't be enough for you to look at the pictures. You'll be able to walk into them, talk with the people they feature, maybe chat with the artist who's lurking behind the most distant wall.

'Life in cyberspace is more egalitarian than elitist, more decentralized than hierarchical ... it serves individuals and communities, not mass audiences. We might think of life in cyberspace as ... founded on the primacy of individual liberty and a commitment to pluralism, diversity, and community.' Mitchell Kapor, creator of Lotus 1-2-3 and co-founder of the Electronic Frontier Foundation, an advocacy group for cyber rights

You will be able to function in Cyberia the way you function in dreams, only better. Anything will be possible. You'll be like Superman, able to use X-ray and microscopic vision, capable of jumping tall buildings in a single bound. You'll be better than Superman. He can't walk through walls without them crashing down, but in Cyberia you can.

Cyberia will allow you to experience reality in a way you've never done before, in a way that wasn't possible before. You might, for example, stand on the cone of an erupting volcano, bathe in a lava flow, breathe at the bottom of the sea, fight sharks (and win), chat up Her Majesty the Queen, catch a bullet with your bare hands, stare into the atomic structure of a flower.

In Cyberia, you will experience computer generated characters as real. You can see them, hear them, touch them. Eventually, I don't doubt you'll be able to taste and smell them too. That means you can discuss philosophy with Socrates, play chess with Ruy Lopez, give advice to the Pope, sing with the Spice Girls.

But don't forget Cyberia is the virtual reality of the Internet, so the people you meet in there won't all be computer simulations. When you visit, the computer will generate a perfect three-dimensional image of you in the relevant location ... and perfect three-dimensional images of everybody else who happens to be visiting at the same time.

Site 52 — Alternative futures

> 'Electric technology is reshaping and restructuring every aspect of our personal life. It is forcing us to reconsider and re-evaluate practically every thought, every action and every institution formerly taken for granted. You, your family, your education, your neighbourhood, your government, your relation to 'the others'. And they're changing dramatically.' Marshal McLuhan, in his book – The Medium is the Massage, 1967.

▶Quantum physicists are beginning to suspect our common sense picture of an unfolding future is just plain wrong.

Einstein's Theory of Relativity showed it was a mistake to consider Space and Time as two different things. Although we experience them as separate, there are in fact simply different aspects of a single Space-time Continuum. Relativity also showed there must be at least one other Space-time Continuum existing on the 'other side' so to speak of Black Holes.

Quantum mechanics went further. Experiments and calculations indicated not just one but an infinite number of parallel universes, all but one theoretically accessible from our own.

But some physicists speculate that our continuum actually interacts with the others. This means that we slip in and out of parallel universes all the time without ever realizing we are doing so. These universes represent the differing potentials for our future. For each of us, an infinite number of alternate futures are waiting. We somehow select the ones we want to live in.

Whether or not this theory is correct, it is quite clear that humanity is today standing at a crossroads where the future of the Internet is concerned. Like nuclear weapons, the Internet will not go away.

But what sort of future it will help us build is far from certain.

Brave new world? Site 53 ▶
Brave new nightmare? Site 54 ▶
The doomsday scenario Site 55 ▶

THE INTERNET

Site 53 — Future perfect

▶Here's a typical day in the life of a student of tomorrow: **Wireheading**[P.171] has become a reality. Your connection with the **Internet**[P.18] is permanent and perfect. You have instant access to **Cyberia** [P.172] at all times using no more than a coded eyeblink.

You can go to school or work without leaving your home ... which means you can work anywhere on earth. In Cyberia you'll have the opportunity of learning from the best lecturers in the world. But you won't be confined to listening to them in some stuffy hall.

You're studying comparative religion and today's subject is Tibetan Buddhism. You enter Cyberia and head for the lecture that's being given by the Dalai Lama. You exchange scarves, say 'hi' to your fellow students, then squat down as the lecture begins.

At first the Dalai Lama only talks to you about Tibet, but after this introduction he decides to show you. So he levitates up out of his chair and leads the whole class on a flight through the window towards the distant Himalayas. Soon you're wandering round the mystic confines of a high Tibetan temple, spinning the prayer wheels and listening to the deep soulful sounds of the chanting monks.

> *'Education must shift into the future tense.'* – **Alvin Toffler in Future Shock.**

By the time he's finished with you, you don't just know about Tibetan Buddhism in theory. You've actually *lived* it.

Cyberia is going to work wonders for your love life.

Nowadays few people are confined to romance with the boy or girl next door, but it's still true to say most relationships are formed within the same village, town or city and certainly within the same country. With the new interface that's set to change. You've now got the whole world to choose from – or at least that healthy proportion of the world that's wired.

Don't forget that in Cyberia you can see, hear and touch. When somebody appears, it's as if he or she was actually there. More importantly, to them it's as if you were actually there. No matter that your physical body is in Luton while hers is in Afghanistan. In Cyberia, you're together.

You have control of the computer image you project. This is already happening with the use of **avatars** P.165. But in virtual reality, your avatar is you. You can lose the spots before you go out on a date. You can grow a little taller, flatten your stomach, change the colour of your eyes, lengthen your legs or grow fur.

The plain, mind-blowing fact is that life in Cyberia is limited only by the available computing power and your imagination. The drug problem has withered and died. Who needs E when you can do anything you've ever wanted, walk inside the confines of a single human cell, touch the double helix of your own DNA, fly across the galaxy at the speed of light, speak with your favourite filmstar, take the trip of a lifetime on the Cyberian Net?

Wireheading means you can stroll into Cyberia from any place at any time. But it also means the real world will become a far more interesting – and controllable – place than it used to be.

Your Cyberian interface will constantly monitor your body functions, quietly checking them against medical parameters in an Internet database. Equally unnoticed, it will make the necessary adjustments to maintain your health and keep your mind and mood at optimum efficiency.

You may have a little digital clock ticking away at the edge of your vision so you always know what time it is.

You will never be lost for a fact to back up your opinions. For the past decade and more, a man named Ted Nelson has been working on a project called Xanadu which is a single database that will contain ... absolutely everything there is to know about anything.

There's still some controversy about whether such a database is even possible. But the project has the backing of some very sober corporations. Ted Nelson himself is no crank. He's the man who invented hypertext, the support system of the **World Wide Web** P.48.

Even if Nelson does not succeed, you will be headwired into a multiplicity of databases that will carry all the information you will ever need. While the physical world may not be as wild as Cyberia, you will certainly be able to cope with it a great deal better than you do today because your interface with the Net will give you more physical control.

On the Internet today, you can link up to a remote robot and cause it to perform simple tasks like picking up objects and setting them down. It's no more than an amusing novelty at the moment, but the implications of the technology are obvious. What the Net has done already is extend your physical reach halfway across the world.

Improve the technology and even outside Cyberia, you will function like a god.

Will it happen? Site 57 ▶

COMING SOON

Site 54 — Future imperfect

▶ Here's a typical day in the life of a student of tomorrow:

Wireheading P.171 has become a reality. Your connection with the Internet is permanent, perfect ... and compulsory.

The New World Government (as the United States of Japan now insists on calling itself) used concern over **pornography** P.126 to justify tighter and tighter controls over the Internet itself and eventually developed *Monitron*, the revolutionary software that tracks the activities of every computer worldwide ... and closes it down instantly if the user is engaged in illegal activity.

With the Net no longer a centre of free discussion and interchange of ideas, the authorities set about converting it into a tool for the control of populations. At first this meant only that every Net server was dedicated to the output of Government propaganda.

Later, with the development of the neural interface, control became tighter.

> *'Picture the future as a jackboot stamping on the human face ... forever!'* – George Orwell in his book 1984.

Even in the twentieth century, neurology was aware of a pleasure centre in the human brain. Early experiments on rats showed the creatures would self stimulate this area in preference to food or sex and literally starve to death in the process. When the ability to stimulate this centre in humans was linked into the new Net interface, the ability to control became absolute.

Shortly after you rise at 6 a.m., your morning oath of allegiance to the World Government is rewarded by a micro-jolt of your pleasure centre. Following breakfast, your **virtual reality Internet connection** P.163 is automatically activated and you join your group in the People's Hyperspace Hall for your first indoctrination session of the day.

Your interface constantly monitors your brain wave patterns and delivers a painful jolt of electricity each time your attention wanders. But you have learned to concentrate so you seldom suffer this indignity and pain.

The indoctrination session ends with a short examination with each expression of politically correct opinion rewarded by a microburst into your pleasure centre. You do particularly well today so you leave your morning session with a blissful smile on your face.

Time now to go to work. Your Personal People's Essential Employment Centre is physically located near Chernobyl in the Eastern European State of the World Federation. The area is still devastated by nuclear radiation, but you do not, of course, have to go there personally.

What actually happens is that you enter an area of hyperspace which allows you to control the robot machinery creating the biological weapons manufactured there. The site has been chosen by your leaders since the radiation levels encourage mutations in the viruses being developed as part of their vital defence strategy.

To your virtual eyes, your environment is a pleasant sylvan setting with sweet music playing in the background as you work the controls and make the decisions that will create ever more virulent strains of Ebola and Marburg. Good decisions – that is, decisions which lead to the results required by the World Government – are rewarded by stimulation of your pleasure centre.

You work throughout the day without any of the meal breaks that so disrupted production in the bad old days before the World Government invented the Internet. Your need for nourishment is monitored by the Net which feeds you intravenously each time your blood sugar drops below optimum levels.

The same mechanism drip-feeds you stimulants that enable you to work a full twenty-hour day. There are rumours of new drugs that will allow you to contribute to society around the clock.

Even now the strictness of the work regime ensures that you will die young. But that does not matter. So long as you maintain the specified levels of output and concentrate on your indoctrination sessions, you will lead a blissful life.

Besides, there are plenty more where you came from.

Will it happen?   Site 57 ▶

Site 55 — Future possible

▶In his short story *The Machine Stops*, the distinguished British novelist E. M. Forster predicted a world in which humanity lived in separate cells of a massive subterranean beehive, never meeting face to face and with all their needs met by a planetary machine.

The development of the Internet has meant that, for the first time in history, such a future has become technically possible.

The seeds are already there. A whole generation of young people has been drawn towards computerized games both at home and in the arcades. Many of them are as much head games as games of skill, allowing players to sink deeper and deeper into a fantasy world.

The **addictive quality of fantasy** P.143 has to be accepted. So has **computer addiction** P.157. It's easy to predict more and more people may become involved in their own fantasy worlds at the expense of day-to-day reality.

In present day terms the great worry about this is that if it goes too far there's no one left to do the essential jobs. But if the development of robotics ever escalates to the same extent as the Net, this problem may disappear.

Should that day come, Forster's vision could become a reality. **Virtual reality** P.163 would allow people to 'travel' and communicate without ever leaving their homes. A neural interface with the Net would monitor their health, nourishment and even exercise needs, which would then be met by robot servants.

As connection with the Net continued to spread, first the developed world, then the world as a whole would sink into Forster's beehive existence. Although there would be those who would speak out against the trend in its early days, there would be just enough practical arguments to support the addictive appeal.

In the fantasy world of virtual reality, competition would wither and die. Anyone could be anything they wanted, could do anything they wanted. Psychopaths would slaughter computer simulations without doing anybody any real harm. Industrialists could amass untold (if largely imaginary) wealth without polluting the planet. With an infinite amount of real estate available in hyperspace, **territorial conflicts** P.116 would become unnecessary. Indeed all war would quickly become obsolete since the ideas and ideologies that cause them could be harmlessly indulged in **Cyberia** P.172.

So, gradually, the human race would become immersed in its own collective fantasies, withdrawing more and more from the real world, relying more and more on its robotic servants and the Net.

Very few would ever recall the actual message of Forster's story: if the human race relies for everything on a great machine, what happens when the machine breaks down?

Could it happen? Site 57 ▶

Section Twelve
IT'S MAKE YOUR MIND UP TIME

It's make your mind up time

Site 56 — Decision Day

➤ Is the Internet a good thing or a bad thing, an example of **Frankenstein technology** P.77 or an exercise in **electronic democracy** P.81?

You will find people queuing up to tell you what to think about this tricky question. There are fundamentalist preachers convinced that the Net is supervised by Satan and starry-eyed idealists who believe it is the salvation of humanity. Once you get involved, you can listen to argument and counter-argument until your head spins.

Sooner or later you will realize that the only thing to do is conduct your own investigation of the Net and make your mind up on that basis. The sites that follow represent a broad cross-section of what's now available on the Net. They include the good, the bad and the ugly. Visit those that interest you, follow a few threads and links. Before you know it you'll be well-equipped to reach Decision Day.

Art

You may be the next da Vinci, but Leonardo never had the sort of help that's available to you at:

http://www.herron.iupui.edu/faculty/larmann/chalk.html.

While you're in the mood, check out:

http://persona.www.media.mit.edu/1010/Exhibit/ (electronic gallery)
http://home.dti.net/shadow/imagesoup/ (computer art)
http://minuteman.com/spiderman/ (Spiderman)

Hobbies

Short of ideas on what to do when you power down your computer? How about learning to juggle at:

http://www.juggling.org/

learning the Tarot at:

http://www2.dgsys.com/~bunning/top.html or

learning how to cook with Kellogg's Rice Krispies (honest!) at:

THE INTERNET

http://www.treatsrecipes.com/ ? Others to look at:
http://www.hcc.hawaii.edu/dinos/dinos.1.html
http://www.windows.umich.edu/
http://fox.nstn.ca/~puppets/index.html

Movies

Every big budget current movie now has its promotional page on **World Wide Web** P.48, but you'll have to search them out for yourself since information would be out of date by the time you read this book. Meanwhile you can get up to date by heading for:

http://www.movieweb.co.uk/frame1.html

where you'll find listings of the latest at your local cinema. Other sites to check are:

http://www.eonline.com/Hot/Features/Russell/
http://www.iguide.com/movies/
http://www.warwick.ac.uk/~miapd/gunge/gunge.html

Music

Your favourite group almost certainly has a Web page, if not a full-fledged fan club, on the Net. Use one of the search sites to find them. Apart from that, pointing your browser at:

http://concerts.calendar.com/

will provide you with an almost unbelievable guide to current gigs worldwide. Punk outposts worth a visit are:

tahoma.cwu.edu:2000/~gossardr/dk_html/dk.html
www.contrib.andrew.cmu.edu/~colon/index.html

Other music sites of interest are:

http://www.rockmine.music.co.uk/Cyclo.html (rock)
http://www.orchestranet.co.uk/ (classical)
http://www.jazzheads.com/site/ (jazz)

School help

You may head for the Net to get away from school, but the fact is there's more help for your homework waiting out there in cyberspace than you'd ever have believed possible. You won't need this stuff all the time, but when you need it you *really* need it:

Ancient Egypt:
http://eyelid.ukonline.co.uk/ancient/egypt.htm
Ancient Greece:
http://www.perseus.tufts.edu/
Grammar:
http://www.nuff.ox.ac.uk/users/martin/languagelive.html
Maths:
http://www.dircon.co.uk/mathline
Science:
http://www.best.com:80/~funsci/
Technology:
http://www.rmplc.co.uk/eduweb/sites/trinity/techhome.html

Sport

Every sport that interests you is represented on the Net. A good place to start is:
http://susis.ust.hk/~danny/sport/europe.html
which will give you links with all (or most) of your favourites. Sport for the disabled is extensively covered at:
http://www.sover.net/~vass/.

Others to look out for:
Gymnastics http://rainbow.rmii.com/~rachele/gymnhome.html
Boxing http://www.boxingonline.com/
Cricket http://www.bogo.co.uk/starter/ashes.html
Soccer http://www.csn.net/~eid/soccer/sccrindx.html
Skateboarding
http://web.cps.msu.edu/~dunhamda/dw/dansworld.html

Seriously weird

Some of these sites defy description. Just try them:
http://fly.hiwaay.net/~lkseitz/comics/herogen/herogen.cgi
http://www.easttexas.com/pdlg/theball.html
http://bronte.cs.utas.edu.au/monkey/
http://www.steveconley.com/supermarketing.html

THE INTERNET

> Site 57 — The last word

▶Nothing has been hyped so much in the last ten years as the Internet.

It's been hailed as the ultimate democracy, a step forward in evolution, a herald of freedom, an opportunity for growth.

It's been slammed as a danger to society, a source of **pornography** P.126, a **terrorist weapon** P.116, a threat to authority.

The Internet is, of course, all these things and more.

The nearest thing to Internet technology that humanity has so far experienced was the invention of the **printing press** P.75.

Printing brought knowledge to more people in more countries than had ever been possible before. It led directly to an expansion of technology (by making technical manuals more widely available). It challenged existing authority. It helped the interchange of information. It enabled different cultures to learn more about each other. It stimulated creativity and generated new sources of wealth.

But printing had its dark side. Among the very first publications of the printing press were pornographic books. It quickly became the world's most effective tool for mind control. It was – and is – a means of spreading lies. In Nazi Germany, Hitler's hate-filled *Mein Kampf* outsold the Bible and Propaganda Minister Goebbels' first act was to take control of the print media. It encouraged conformity on a mass scale.

Even now, in the relatively early stages of its development, it is easy to see the Internet is following much the same pattern.

> '*I want to discuss another dinosaur, one that may be on the road to extinction. I am referring to the American media and I use the term extinction literally. To my mind, it is likely that what we now understand as the mass media will be gone within ten years. Vanished, without a trace.*' – Michael Crichton, best-selling author.

But the potential of the Internet is greater by far than the potential of printing. The key to this potential is interaction. Unlike all other media, the user of the Internet is always *involved*.

It is this involvement that makes the Internet so dangerous ... and at the same time gives the greatest cause for hope.

The Internet today is far from perfect. It is lively, opinionated, silly, immoral, greedy, joyful, courageous, crusading, honest and dishonest by turns. In other words it's human – the one invention in the history of our species that most closely mirrors ourselves.

The Internet may yet prove to be **Frankenstein technology** P.77 like the chemical industries that pollute our rivers, the fossil fuel machinery that is warming the globe, the nuclear weaponry that threatens planetary survival. But only if humanity itself is a Frankenstein monster, bent on self-destruction.

You've read the arguments pro and con throughout this book. You've probably experienced something of the Internet itself by now. You've read the brief summary of arguments in this final site. Now's the time for you to do a little thinking.

THE INTERNET

For better or for worse, the future of the Internet is in your hands. It will become exactly what you make it.

Log off.